HUMAN EVOLUTION
A SPIRITUAL-SCIENTIFIC QUEST

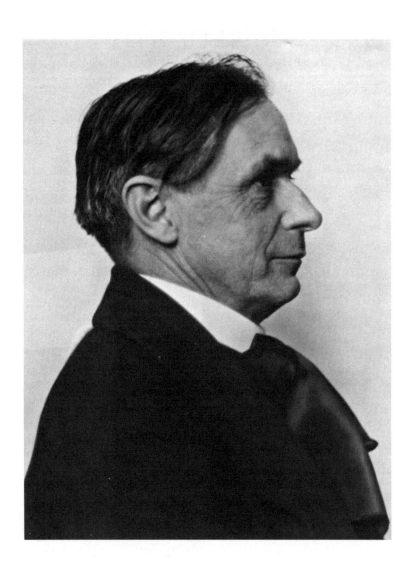

HUMAN EVOLUTION
A SPIRITUAL-SCIENTIFIC QUEST

Nine lectures held in Dornach between 17 August and 2 September 1918

TRANSLATED BY SIMON BLAXLAND-DE LANGE

INTRODUCTION BY SIMON BLAXLAND-DE LANGE

RUDOLF STEINER

RUDOLF STEINER PRESS

CW 183

The publishers gratefully acknowledge the generous funding of this publication by the estate of Dr Eva Frommer MD (1927–2004) and the Anthroposophical Society in Great Britain

Rudolf Steiner Press
Hillside House, The Square
Forest Row, RH18 5ES

www.rudolfsteinerpress.com

Published by Rudolf Steiner Press 2014

Originally published in German under the title *Die Wissenschaft vom Werden des Menschen* (volume 183 in the *Rudolf Steiner Gesamtausgabe* or Collected Works) by Rudolf Steiner Verlag, Dornach. Based on shorthand transcripts not reviewed by the speaker, and edited by Johann Waeger, Robert Friedenthal and Susi Loetscher. This authorized translation is based on the latest available edition (1990)

Published by permission of the Rudolf Steiner Nachlassverwaltung, Dornach

ISBN 978 1 85584 405 6

Cover by Mary Giddens
Typeset by DP Photosetting, Neath, West Glamorgan
Printed and bound by Gutenberg Press, Malta

CONTENTS

zone lies a conscious inner space. The other zone corresponds to the power of love; and beyond this zone is the soul-spiritual aspect of the universe.

LECTURE 3
DORNACH, 19 AUGUST 1918

The Aims of the Initiates of the East, of the West and of Jesuitism. The Demonic Influence of Ahriman upon Mankind through Technology

The two boundary zones of man's soul being. Before the fourth post-Atlantean epoch one of these thresholds was still permeable; the other one will be in the sixth epoch. Something is already now beginning to seep through, rising up from within. This must be harmonized. Eastern and western cultural impulses (Tagore, Wilson). The different aims of oriental initiates and of the initiates of Americanism. The oriental impulse of abandoning the earthly human race. The American impulse of becoming strongly immersed in one's bodily nature. The growth of an ahrimanic, demonic quality within humanity through technology. Salvation through the spirit of Christ and an understanding of spiritual-scientific knowledge.

LECTURE 4
DORNACH, 24 AUGUST 1918

The Threefold Sun Mystery of Ancient Times. The Mystery of Christ Jesus and of the Threefold Being of Man

The natural order and the moral order. The connection of Christ with the Sun mystery. The transformation of man's powers of imagination necessary in order to understand the dualism Christ-Jesus. The mystery of threefold man. Threefold man as a reflection of his archetypal image. The dualism between truth and science and how it may be overcome.

LECTURE 5

DORNACH, 25 AUGUST 1918

The Nature of Threefold Man. The Twelve Senses. Socialism. Apollonius of Tyana

The shape of the head as the physical manifestation of an ancient form goes back to ahrimanic principles; the spiritual aspect of the head is a youthful form. The principles of earthly development are active mainly in the region of the trunk. The luciferic formative principles of the limbs will have their full development only in the Venus existence of the Earth. The human individuality needs to be viewed both from a cosmic and also from a human standpoint. The significance of the subconsciousness, which has become veiled, and whose various stages must in our time once again be recovered by the human consciousness. The senses. Intersection of the streams in the middle region of man's being. Memory, cosmic tableau and microcosmic aura. The inverted senses. The parallel between microcosmic man and the cosmic alternation of day and night. Such concepts which connect the life of nature and spiritual life encompass what can work fruitfully in social and historical life, whereas the mechanistic world-conception has led mankind into chaos.

LECTURE 6

DORNACH, 26 AUGUST 1918

The Human Soul in Relation to the Soul World. The Limbs as Thoughts of the Higher Hierarchies. The Loss of the Spiritual Knowledge of the Old Mysteries

Burning questions which can never be answered with the means available to the modern age, for the imaginative conceptions of spiritual and earthly man have been lost. The deceptive quality of the physical Sun. Empty space and negative materiality; the concept of less than empty. Holes in the brain as a tool of the life of the soul, which comes up against the substance of the brain and is reflected there. After a person's death this then becomes a conscious experience for him. The human aura with its streams that constitute his soul-life, which is formed from the elements of the soul-world. After death a person thereby enters into a certain relationship with the soul-world and the spirit-land. Those elements become free and are transformed; in this way the soul-life is hollowed out and the spiritual life emerges. The conditions of transformation. The idea of metamorphosis can be made fruitful for an understanding of man's transition from one incarnation to another. The physical world exists through the interweaving of the thoughts of the higher hierarchies, of formative thoughts into material thoughts. Such clearly expressed concepts of the old mysteries must be experienced anew through spiritual science. The schematic drawing of the old Pythagorean Schools. The legacy of abstract concepts from ancient Rome through the Middle Ages into modern times. As a result of this man was lost in the nineteenth century, and was rediscovered from the aspect of his animal nature. This situation has created the gulf and the catastrophic realities associated with it. The rudiments for understanding man's spiritual being lie in the ideas of metamorphosis.

LECTURE 7
DORNACH, 31 AUGUST 1918

The Gulf Between Idealism and Realism. The Formation of Language from Cosmic Intelligence

Relationship of morality and ideas with natural events. The illusory nature of the outer physical world. The gulf between idealism and realism and the split inherent in our intellectual life, brought about by the naturalistic way in which we behold the world and the moral nature of our idealism. Our living connection with the cosmic reason or intelligence, discernible in the creative formulation of ideas in language. Its reduction by the dead into its component parts. The place of eurythmy in the whole process of human evolution.

LECTURE 8
DORNACH, 1 SEPTEMBER 1918

The Pythagorean School and the Mendacity of the World at that Time. The Disintegration of Words after Death. The Members of a Dead Person's Being

The appearance of a radical untruthfulness in certain historical epochs; investigation of the context. The Pythagorean School and the world surrounding it. Emergent and destructive forces. The atomizing of words after death. Unveiling of the spiritual significance of death. Disintegration of the inexpressible Name of God. As the word is reduced to the vowels of which it is composed the spiritual element is revealed out of the process of disintegration. As the sound of the word fades away the soul sees the spiritual world shine forth. Spiritualization after death.

The members of man's being in the spiritual world between death and a new birth. The orientating and death-bringing cosmic power of the hierarchies. The disenchantment of the soul-realm. The cosmic power of the dissolution of form.

pages 119–131

LECTURE 9

DORNACH, 2 SEPTEMBER 1918

Time and Space. The Perspectivity of Time. The Influence of Ahriman and Lucifer upon Man

The nature of time by analogy with space. Man experiences only the image of real time. Earlier periods of time relate to the present in a perspective-like way. The similarity of time to space and its constant link with all that is. In nature Ahriman works from the past. Man follows the course of time and does not notice the perspective of time; the consequence is that ahrimanic powers are able to work within him as a present reality; by this means man separates his present existence from the spiritual domain. That he cherishes ideals is the consequence of the luciferic powers that he bears within him, powers that endeavour to tear him away from nature and spiritualize him. The balance lies in the unconscious regions of man's being; at present it is created through the early death of children and young people. The death of old people makes the physical Earth more spiritual than it would be otherwise. Transformation of human forms from soul-spiritual existence into their earthly human counterparts: of the head as a result of ahrimanic influences, of the limbs through luciferic influences. In the region of the chest: influence of normally evolved divine beings through the living breath. Here is also the dividing wall, our memory, through which in this threefold picture the ahrimanic powers of the head are kept separate from the luciferic powers of the extremities, and prevent a connection between the natural order and the spiritual order from taking place within us.

pages 132–157

INTRODUCTION

It is apparent from a number of statements in the course of these lectures that Dornach was where Rudolf Steiner most wanted to be at this time. The work on the first Goetheanum and the sculptural Group, which he regarded as a wholly constructive deed amidst the chaos that continued to engulf Europe, formed a central part of his creative activity. And yet he had been away from Switzerland—where he had spent the whole of the previous autumn—since 20 January 1918 and only returned to Dornach on or around 12 August, shortly before giving the course of lectures contained in this volume. He clearly considered this year to represent a crucial opportunity to try to influence the cultural and social affairs of the German heartland in such a way that a threefold conception of the social organism based on a spiritual view of man could supplant a determination to mount a military offensive; and it was for this reason that Berlin—where he had journeyed with Marie Steiner on 20 January—was the city to which he constantly returned during this last year of the war and where all the lecture cycles (though not by any means all the lectures) during this period were given.

However, the mustering of spiritual forces that characterized this period of absence from Dornach was also marked by intensive work on producing newly revised and augmented editions of several of his basic books (he did not write any new books during this time). A notable instance of this work concerned the thorough revisions of his major philosophical book *The Philosophy of Freedom*; but he also produced new editions of *Goethe's World View*, *Theosophy*, *A Road to Self-Knowledge*, *The Threshold of the Spiritual World* and *The Riddles of Philosophy*. Just before giving the lectures included in CW 183 he had been working on a new edition of *An Outline of Occult Science*, which was to appear only in the middle of 1920, not long before the first Goetheanum fully opened as a centre for lectures and courses on 26 September 1920.

This period of outward concern for and involvement with the tragic conflict raging in Europe, coupled with an intense recalibration of the principal source-books of anthroposophy, was reflected in what Rudolf Steiner brought by means of these lectures to his closest colleagues, his 'home audience', in Dornach shortly after the middle of August 1918. On the one hand he brings tidings of his travels, his impressions and thoughts, together with a clear, critical judgement of a world in turmoil and bereft of any clarity of direction; and on the other he plunges into a renewed analysis of the esoteric work that this outward world-situation requires from the Anthroposophical Society and the community associated with it. Indeed, the scope of the inner content of these lectures goes so far as to encompass certain essential aspects of the Lessons of the First Class of the School of Spiritual Science, which Rudolf Steiner was to give in the entirely new circumstances of the anthroposophical movement that prevailed in 1924. However, it is doubtful whether his listeners were able at the time to appreciate the full meaning of these deeply esoteric lectures. This observation is prompted by the fact that the blackboard drawings, through which much of the esoteric content was transmitted (somewhat akin to the mantras of the First Class), were not preserved in the form in which they were given. A further issue in this regard is that the integrity of this course as a cycle of nine lectures (as opposed to three groups of three lectures, which is how they were made available until 1967 in German and until now in English) cannot have been clearly perceived at the time. In the brief introductory survey that follows, an attempt will be made to give some idea of the themes running through the entire cycle of lectures.

After an introductory lecture in which Rudolf Steiner gives a stark and incisive impression of the prevailing state of cultural life in the context of the catastrophic conditions of war-torn Europe, together with an indication of the longing for a more spiritual understanding of life (a general diagnosis which, especially in terms of the 'three basic evils in present-day human culture' to which he refers, seems no less true today than it was at the time), he plunges in the second lecture without further ado into contrasting the state of separateness that a physical human being experiences with respect to his environment with the active involvement of his aura, or his soul-spiritual being, in his cosmic surroundings; and we are made aware of the inner and outer thresholds within which life in a physical human body is enacted, together with the boundaries that both limit and protect the integrity of this physical human existence. In the third lecture there is a clear presentation of the need in our time to penetrate both these boundaries or to cross the threshold into the spiritual world, while being very fully aware of the immense dangers inherent in, respectively, narrowly eastern and western cultural impulses which would in different ways render further human evolution on Earth impossible (warnings that are even more pertinent in the early 21st century than they were at the time).

With these three lectures as a background, Rudolf Steiner now introduces in the fourth lecture what could be described as the underlying theme of the whole cycle, namely, the dualism, or gulf, between the divine and human world, on the one hand, and the world of nature on the other (or, in the somewhat neater German formulation, between *Geisteswissenschaft* and *Naturwissenschaft*), between ideas and ideals and the domain of science and technology, and also between the cosmic Christ and the earthly Jesus; and we are shown by way of a striking image how our threefold human form, which while existing in space also lives in the dimension of time, reflects the full archetypal dimension of man as a spiritual being and therefore also represents the key to overcoming this duality in all its various aspects. (The seminal importance of the research in the previous year that had led, after thirty years of quiet reflection, to Rudolf Steiner's observations regarding the threefold nature of the human soul in relation to the bodily organism can hardly be overestimated.) In the next two lectures this relationship of our threefold human form is placed in the context of, on the one hand, the evolutionary journey of our human individuality from the past through the present and into the far future and, on the other, the soul-world of the human aura as described in the second lecture; and towards the end of the sixth lecture we are presented with a clear analysis of how the understanding of these matters that still resided in the Pythagorean Schools of ancient Greece was lost amidst the abstract concepts developed in ancient Rome and that there was by the nineteenth century a distinct possibility of losing all understanding of man's true being:

These states of consciousness have become more or less veiled since the beginning of the fourth post-Atlantean epoch, since 747 BC. The challenge of our time is to summon forth the specific awareness of these various processes of cosmic and human evolution from the general chaos of human consciousness today. [Lecture 5]

This theme of the gulf between what may loosely be referred to as idealism and realism (the world of ideas and the reality of the sense-perceptible world of nature) is then, in the seventh lecture, developed into what is currently an existential reality for a humanity that is confronted by the threat of global warming and the potential destruction of the material Earth which is the foundation of our human existence. Language is referred to as a last living vestige of the true relationship between physical earthly life and the spiritual world that— as soul-spiritual beings—we enter after death; and the eighth lecture develops this theme of the origin of language in relation to cultural evolution in the context of the soul's journey after death in the spiritual world. The concluding ninth lecture contains a lengthy passage of some sixteen pages which demonstrates how a failure to be aware of perspective in the dimension of time is responsible for the obdurate persistence of what Owen Barfield refers to as the 'idols' of sense-perceptible phenomena, together with the assumption that human consciousness has always perceived the same world and that something of the nature of an evolution of that consciousness is a figment of the fanciful imagination. The main additional thrust of this lecture is to show how crucial it is that the illusions that Ahriman and Lucifer have (legitimately and with important positive consequences) fostered in human consciousness are overcome in our time and that abstract scientific theories about the nature of reality, on the one hand, and ideas devoid of any capacity to work right into this earthly reality in a spiritually transforming way, must as a matter of urgency give place to a true knowledge of man as a being of soul and spirit as has been described over the course of this whole cycle of lectures. That is to say, there needs to be an awareness that 'every ideal is a seed for a future event in nature; every natural event is the fruit of a spiritual event [that is, an event wrought by "the divine and human world"} in the past'. Rudolf Steiner also emphasizes that the measures described in the lecture that have hitherto been put in place by the good Gods to maintain some sort of connection between earthly existence between birth and death and the world between death and a new birth will no longer be adequate to prevent a catastrophic parting of the ways.

Running though this cycle of lectures—but especially in the seventh and ninth lectures—is an affirmation of the importance of the contribution that the Anthroposophical Society and the anthroposophical movement can make to this process, together with an awareness that there have been many failures in this respect, especially in connection with a tendency towards sectarianism and dogmatic judgements. What is so striking is that in this and in so many other ways Rudolf Steiner's insights seem no less relevant to our own century than they were to the time when he was speaking.

Simon Blaxland-de Lange, July 2014

LECTURE 1

As you may imagine, it gives me the deepest satisfaction to be able once more to begin working amongst you on, and in the vicinity of, this building of ours.[1] Indeed, anyone who has come in contact with the whole aura of this building today—not only through a deep study of it but even through a more superficial understanding—may become aware that something is associated with this building which has a connection with the most significant and momentous future tasks of mankind. Especially after my prolonged enforced absence[2] you may be sure that I have a profound sense of satisfaction to be once again in this place where this building stands as a symbol of our cause.

I should also like to emphasize that, every time that I return after a long absence, I have a particular satisfaction from being able to see how well and how meaningfully the work on this building is being nurtured by the devoted service of those who are actively engaged on it. Especially in these months of my last absence, when work has been undertaken in such difficult circumstances, certain aspects of the artistic work have progressed in an incomparable way and in the spirit that needs to pervade it in its entirety.

But I am also deeply gratified to see that the spirit of our work and of what is coming into being here has led to a real sense of solidarity among many of our friends and a true devotion to what this building embodies. And as one dwells upon this fact, one comes to see that here we have a place which is associated with convictions of such sincerity on the part of a number of friends of our spiritual movement that they give one the assurance that the best impulses of our spiritual movement will flow into the future of humanity, where they are so deeply needed. In the work devoted to this building, there is already something that could serve as a model for all that is intended by what we refer to today as the Anthroposophical Society.[3]

On the other hand, however, I often have the feeling that the beneficial and essentially good aspect of what is found here in this building as a result of human work and human feeling consists in this building's objective capacity to free what is wanted by our movement from the subjective interests of individual human beings.

Regarding what has just been touched upon here, some remarkable views have been—and are still being—expressed in all societies of this nature, and equally in the Anthroposophical Society itself, which are actually remarkable illusions. People preach a lot about selflessness and universal human love; but this is often merely a mask for certain subtle egotistical interests emanating from individual human beings. It is true that these people do not know that their interests are of a purely egotistical nature, and that as regards their individual consciousness they are in a certain sense innocent; but nevertheless this is how things stand. However, the building demands from a relatively large number of our friends a selfless devotion to something objective, to something standing as a symbol of our cause that is free from any particular personality; and to that extent what is connected with our building can indeed serve as a model for what our movement seeks to become.

My dear friends, when we greet one another again as we are doing today, we should particularly direct our attention to what is fruitful and all-embracing in this spiritual movement of ours; and as we greet one another in this way we need to give serious consideration to the thought that however it may happen—and the manner in which it will do so will depend on the circumstances—mankind will never extricate itself from the terrible blind alley in which it has become lodged in our present age until the resolve is made in some way to seek a starting point for fruitful activity and fruitful deeds within a spiritual movement such as ours. We shall certainly not insist egotistically that the truth is to be found only within our small confined circle; but we need to be conscious that we are members of a circle where it is recognized that man has got himself into his terrible present predicament by neglecting his spiritual substance. We may recognize ourselves as people who are united with those ideas which can alone lead mankind out of the blind alley where it has now arrived.

There is indeed a great deal in the souls of people today that is lacking in clarity. When it has been possible to refresh our understanding here and there of the needs that currently prevail in the view of our spiritual movement, one can say on the one hand: yes, the number of the souls of those who are thirsting for spiritual life in the way that we have in mind has greatly increased. The longing for such spiritual life can well be said to have become infinitely greater; and the attention given to our impulses has also undeniably become greater in recent years, at any rate in those spheres that have been outwardly accessible to me in the last few years and especially in recent months. It is, moreover, not without significance if I point out that such an intensifying and strengthening of this longing of human souls for spiritual life has become very clearly manifest. To be sure, this strengthening and sharpening of the longing for spiritual life is in strong contrast to that terrible confusion from which by far the greater part of mankind is suffering—a confusion which is caused by outworn ideas, or, rather, an outworn absence of ideas, a languidness with regard to any keen, vigorous thought, languidness that derives from the laxity, from the indolence with which intellectual life on Earth has been conducted for many decades. This laxity, this indolence, leads people astray in the longing for spiritual life that they experience today. On the one hand, they have a real longing for spirituality, for strong supersensible impulses. On the other hand, they are fettered by all the old forces that do not wish to withdraw from the scene of human activity but should nevertheless be able to see from the contribution that they have made to this very activity that they no longer have a place there. One might say that this dark impression, that impression of a bilateral cleft, is to be found everywhere.

I have given lectures illustrated with slides in a number of places—in Hamburg, Berlin and Munich—about the Group that will stand at the focal point of our building.[4] It has on the one hand been possible to see what powerful impulses enter the souls of those who, because of the circumstances of recent years, have never been able to have a glimpse of what is going on here. A new understanding of man is arising from the very way in which the impulses of Ahriman and Lucifer have been conceived, portrayed and made manifest together with that of Christ through our Group. It grips people's souls when what is thus depicted is presented to them. On the other hand, however, we find everywhere the obstructive influences of the all-pervading remnants of what is old and degenerate in our so-called cultural life.

This could be seen particularly from what one might well call the deeply humorous way in which the lectures were received[5] that I gave at the art centre of our friend Herr von Bernus in Munich,[6] when I was trying to bring the inner impulses underlying the conception of art that we are unfolding here to a wider public. This did arouse a considerable degree of interest among people; for I gave lectures of this kind in Munich in February and in May and had to give each of them twice. Herr von Bernus assured me that there were so many enquiries that each of the public lectures where I presented the principles of my conception of art, as they have found expression here in the building, could have been given four times over. But if one were looking for agreement, one would of course be less pleased by the critic of a Munich newspaper who exhibited what might be called a highly refined form of humorous baring of teeth. It was particularly amusing, since an inner resentment towards what the writer was unable to understand made itself felt. His sentiments were not so much spoken as spat out, if you may forgive the expression. This was made evident by the very interest aroused by the matters under consideration, where honesty and sincerity came to expression in contrast to what otherwise emanated from this artistic centre (for after all this is Munich, the famous Munich). Thus one could see how in this centre of artistic activity both the most intelligible and the most unintelligible things were said. In this very discrepancy there is an example of how the two streams of which I have spoken to you exist in our present time, and how we need to be conscious that we are involved in a struggle of essential importance for the future of the world.

I am certainly not saying all this because I would in some way aim to have a 'good press' when things that matter to us have publicity; for the moment we had a 'good press' I would think there must be something wrong, an untruth must have entered into something that we have done.

All these things make us thoroughly aware that it is very necessary for us to stand resolutely on the ground of our cause; for nothing could lead us into greater confusion than if we sought to make any kind of compromise with what the outer world would consider it right for us to do. Only the principles underlying our cause can give us guidance for what we have to do.

There has recently also been an ever-growing interest in a number of places in eurythmy, which while more indirectly connected with the core of our activities is nevertheless inwardly associated with it. And when we who were present remember how eurythmy, for example, was received in one particular place where it had scarcely been seen before and was to an extent a new experience for those who saw it, namely in Hamburg, this reception of something associated with our cause should be recalled with the deepest satisfaction. It was precisely in Hamburg that it was possible to see the deep significance of the impulses which can likewise spring from a cause such as ours. People were there who were actually witnessing a proper performance of eurythmy for the first time. It will also probably become possible to reach a public audience in this way. But in such a situation we must stand on very firm ground and do nothing that is not wholly consistent with our cause. It would otherwise very soon be seen that if things go beyond a certain point people would be rash to suppose that I am prepared to be flexible over matters that I am personally involved with. Most of you already know that I am of course always ready to go along with everyone in every respect where the point at issue is not a matter of principle but where a purely human concern has come to the fore. However, when it is a question of approaching the threshold where a matter of principle would have—even in the smallest degree—to be denied, I shall show myself to be inflexible. Thus at the present time, when there is so much dancing to be seen (for there is dancing everywhere, it is quite dreadful; if you live in a city you could watch dancing displays every evening), if it should be thought—and I have good reason to say this, although I am not referring to any specific instance—that by giving public performances of eurythmy we had the intention of allying ourselves with a journalistic empty-headedness that makes claims for attention, I would protest against this in the most vigorous way possible. A feeling for what is good taste needs to arise solely out of the cause that we share.

Sometimes we also have to remember, especially when we meet one another again, to do what is needful with a fine-tuned will in accordance with our spiritual impulses. These spiritual impulses will have much to fight against. It is no longer enough merely to speak of prejudice, for these forces work too strongly to be encompassed by such a weak term; suffice it to say that these impulses have much to battle with. I have on several occasions referred to the great sickness of our time, which consists in a lack of control over one's thought life. For the activity of thinking is already in itself a spiritual life, when rightly understood. It is because people have so little regard for their life of thinking that they so seldom find their way into the spiritual worlds. Again and again I find it necessary to say from a variety of different aspects that people give an unbelievably great consideration to the mere content of thoughts. But the content of thoughts is what is of the least importance about them. True, a grain of wheat is a grain of wheat, that is indisputable. But even though a grain of wheat is a grain of wheat, when you put it into good, fertile ground you obtain a lush ear of wheat; if you put it into ground that is barren and stony, you either get nothing at all or a very poor specimen. But on each occasion you are dealing with a grain of wheat.

Let us speak of something other than grains of wheat. Instead of a grain of wheat let us say the 'idea of a free humanity' which is such a topic of conversation today; thus many will say that the 'idea of a free humanity' is the 'idea of a free humanity'. It is just the same as a grain of wheat being a grain of wheat. But it is a different matter whether the 'idea of a free humanity' flourishes in a heart, in a soul where this heart and soul is fertile ground or whether the 'idea of a free humanity'— exactly the same idea with the same foundation—is being nurtured in Woodrow Wilson's head![7] Just as a grain of wheat cannot flourish if it is sown in stony ground or among rocks, all the so-called beautiful ideas that are put forward in the programmes of Woodrow Wilson signify nothing if they come from this head. Especially this is something that modern man finds infinitely difficult to understand, because he is of the view that people relate to the content of programmes, to the content of ideas. But the content of programmes, the content of ideas, has as little significance as the germinating power of a grain of wheat before it is sown in ground which can offer it suitable conditions for growth.

Thinking in accordance with reality is so vitally necessary for people today; for something else is connected with the unreal thinking of the present, namely that people are surprised by almost all that happens. Indeed, one might ask if there is anything that has not surprised humanity in the last few years. People are surprised by everything, and they will continue to be a lot more surprised than they are now. But they will not have anything to do with what is really going on in the world. Hence it is also impossible to persuade people today to bring any foresight to bear on their affairs.

If one is working with mere ideas, one can from any standpoint substantiate everything by means of anything. If one is working with the mere content of ideas, one can indeed substantiate everything with everything. This is also something that increasingly needs to be gone into more and more deeply, but no one really wants to do this.

Generally when one speaks of such things and gives examples, no one really believes what one says because the examples seem so grotesque. But our whole modern cultural life is fairly buzzing with these phenomena which manifest themselves in such grotesque ways. I know that many of you will not take it kindly if I give you a really unusual idea as an example; but this is what I propose to do.

This concerns a university professor,[8] an old well-respected university professor who stumbled upon the fact that, in the course of his long life, Goethe was attracted by various women. So this dawned upon a university professor who had taken on the task of thoroughly studying Goethe's life and the lives of those associated with him. Despite not being a professor at a European university, he has of course made it his business to go about these studies as thoroughly as only a professor at a university in central Europe would normally do: he let the whole gallery of Goethe's ladies pass before his soul in a kind of review in their relationship to Goethe. And what did he discover? I can tell you almost in his very words. He found that each of the women whom Goethe loved for a while during his life can be said to have been a kind of Belgium whose neutrality he violated; and that he then sighed that his heart bled for needing to take advantage of a shining innocence. But he did not forget to assert on each occasion like the German chancellor[9] that the realm of violated neutrality would have deserved a better fate but that he, Goethe, could not have done otherwise, since his destiny and the rights of his intellectual life obliged him to sacrifice the one he loved and, even, to offer up the pain of his own heart on the altar of the duty that he owed to his own immortal ego.

I could regale you with many other bizarre ideas from this book. You would ask what purpose this would serve. But there is a good reason for this, for you find ideas of this sort all over the world today. The ideas of people today are of this nature. And it is not for nothing that such ideas should manifest themselves in literature where the essence of human thinking appears; for this view is represented by Santayana, a professor at Harvard University in America, a well-respected Spaniard who is, however, completely Americanized. His book was written during this present catastrophe, and its French edition was introduced by Boutroux,[10] who had given a great eulogy of German philosophy in Heidelberg shortly before the war. This book is called *Egotism in German Philosophy* [Rudolf Steiner referred to it by the title of its French translation] and its publication was no chance event but is entirely characteristic of present-day thinking; for with a similar ease displayed by Professor Santayana in comparing the violation of Belgian neutrality with Goethe's behaviour towards a number of women do these people of today form a binding connection with what is furthest removed from their true nature. The fact is that, if you really take notice of what is going on, this thinking confronts you in all realms of so-called modern science.

It is the task of those spiritual impulses to which our anthroposophically oriented science of the spirit is dedicated to combat three basic evils in the present so-called culture of present-day humanity. It has no choice but to fight against these three basic evils. One of these basic evils manifests itself in the realm of thinking, another in the realm of feeling, and the third in the realm of the will.

In the realm of thinking we have gradually reached the point where people are only able to think in the manner of a thinking that is bound to the physical brain. But this thinking which is so closely wedded to the physical brain has no wish to soar freely to the spiritual domain and is condemned in all circumstances to be narrow-minded and limited. The most significant symptom of modern scientific thinking is narrow-mindedness, limitation of outlook. To be sure, great things can be achieved in this limited domain, as exemplified by modern science. But no element of genius is needed for science as it is conceived of today. This narrow-mindedness, limitation of outlook is what must be challenged in the intellectual realm. Today my intention is merely to present in outline what we shall speak of later in greater detail.

In the realm of feeling the situation is that people have gradually arrived at a certain philistinism—this is the only word for it: pettiness, philistinism, being confined to certain limited circles. This is the main characteristic of the philistine, that he is incapable of being interested in the wider affairs of the world. Parish-pump politicians are always philistines. Of course this cannot suffice in the realm of spiritual science, for here one cannot limit oneself to a narrow circle. There is even a need for us to be interested in what lies beyond the Earth and, hence, in a very wide circle indeed. It does of course annoy people if someone merely suggests the idea of wanting to know something about wider matters such as the Moon, Sun and Saturn.[11] But philistinism needs to give way in all areas to non-philistinism if spiritual science is to be able to make any mark. Sometimes this is not an easy matter, for it requires an ability unreservedly to face up to the matter at hand and, moreover, in an unprejudiced way.

Recently something rather awkward happened in our midst; but I prevented any serious development of what was potentially present in the situation. As you will recall from my lectures in Zurich last year,[12] among various examples I gave then of how Darwinism can be overcome through scientific investigation itself I referred to the excellent book by Oscar Hertwig,[13] *Das Werden der Organismen* ('How Organisms Come Into Being'). Both now and whenever I have had the opportunity I have mentioned this outstanding book. Very soon after this book was published there appeared a shorter book[14] by this same Oscar Hertwig, where he speaks about social, ethical and political life; and I then thought to myself that it could well happen that some of our members, having heard that I said that Oscar Hertwig's book *Das Werden der*

Organismen is a very fine book, will believe that I regard Oscar Hertwig as an infallible authority. This second publication by Oscar Hertwig is a worthless book, one written by someone who is unable to put together a single coherent thought in the realm of social, ethical and political life. I feared that some of our members might have judged that this book had some merit simply because its author was the same Oscar Hertwig. So I had to anticipate any possible problems by taking hold of any opportunity to draw attention to the fact that I consider this second book by the same author who had written a first-rate scientific book to be a worthless piece of foolish nonsense written by a man who lacks the capacity to speak of what he is addressing here.

Our anthroposophical spiritual science does not allow one to pass idly from one thing to the other without examining the facts anew without prejudice. It demands from people that they carefully consider the actual reality of each individual case. Philistinism is something that will disappear if the impulses of spiritual science become widespread. So much for the realm of feeling.

And in the realm of will there is something that has especially in recent times taken hold of mankind in the widest sense, something that I can only call ineptitude. Because of the limitations of what one learns in a narrow circle, people today are by and large very able within the limits of a narrow circle but somewhat inept with respect to everything outside this circle. One comes across men who can't even sew on a button! Ineptitude outside a very limited circle is what is especially prevalent in the realm of the will.

Anyone who takes hold of what we call spiritual science not with purely abstract thoughts but with his whole being will see that this spiritual science goes right into the dexterity of the hands, that it makes a person more capable and enables him to extend his interest over wider areas and his will over a wider world. Of course spiritual science is still too weak to overcome ineptitude altogether, but the more intensively we cultivate it the more will it be able to deal with this problem.

So I would say that there are three barriers to the acceptance of spiritual science today: narrow-mindedness on the intellectual plane, philistinism—that is, pettiness—in the realm of feeling, and ineptitude in the realm of the will. People love these three qualities today, even if they are not fully conscious of doing so. Nothing in the whole world arouses a greater affection today than ineptitude, philistinism and narrow-mindedness. And because people love these three qualities it is not easy for them to reach forward to the wider vistas that they need to discover, to all that is connected with the names of Ahriman and Lucifer. It is precisely here that there is something important to be understood in our time, for one of the many features of our age is that a very important transition is taking place from the luciferic to the ahrimanic domain. And as this transition comes to manifestation not only elsewhere but also here in Switzerland, one can also speak of it here. In this region the former is perhaps of less significance because of the habitual customs of the Swiss; but the latter shows every prospect of becoming more important in this country. In certain respects mankind is in a process of transition from luciferic to ahrimanic faults, from luciferic impulses running counter to human evolution to ahrimanic counter-impulses.

Certain impulses that formerly held sway in the educational domain were of a thoroughly luciferic nature. In this domain—as we all, with the exception of the youngest of us, knew very well when we were young—one has had to deal with ambition and vanity. Thus one was confronted—perhaps less here in Switzerland but on a fairly broad scale elsewhere in the world—with ambition and vanity, with orders and titles and so forth! The entire life's path of many people was based on these luciferic impulses of vanity and ambition, on being of greater worth than other people. Just try to think back to how educational affairs were indeed founded on such luciferic impulses.

At the present time there is an endeavour to replace these luciferic impulses with ahrimanic ones. They are enshrouded today behind the concept of 'ability tests'.[15] This is the ahrimanic equivalent to the luciferic encouragement of ambition and vanity in the child. The aim today is to seek out the most gifted, those who in any event are most successful in class; and from these certain individuals are selected. Ability tests are then carried out with these children, intelligence tests, memory tests, tests of their powers of comprehension and so on. This is something for which the Swiss have a strong predisposition. Although the luciferic aspect has played a lesser role here, the ahrimanic aspect is already manifesting itself in germinal form in the way these ability tests are understood. For these ability tests proceed from the intellect, from science, from present-day academic psychology. Then those gifted ones who are to be tested are made to sit down, and they are given these written words: *murderer—mirror—murderer's victim*.

And they sit there, poor lambs, in front of the three words murderer, mirror and murderer's victim and they are supposed to look for connecting links between them. One child finds the following link: the murderer is creeping up on his victim, but the victim has a mirror in which the murderer is reflected, and so the victim is able to save himself. So much for the first child; his powers of comprehension enable him to connect the three words.

Now comes another: a murderer is creeping up on his victim and sees himself in a mirror. His face appears to him in the mirror as the face of someone with a bad conscience, and so the murderer leaves the victim alone on account of seeing his face in the mirror. These are the connections made by the second child.

The third child arrives at a different way of combining the words. A murderer is creeping up and finds a mirror. He bangs into it, the mirror falls over and makes a terrible noise as it comes crashing down. The murderer's victim hears this racket and is in time to defend himself against the murderer.

The last child is the cleverest! The first one merely found the most obvious combination of ideas, the second described a related moral aspect, while the third has found a very complicated connection of ideas. He is the most gifted! Well, this is more or less how it goes. One is expected to add a little colouring of one's own when making even only a brief description. But this is how children's abilities are going to be tested to find out those who are most able.

One thing is certain: if those who invented these methods were to think of the great people whom they revere, such as Helmholtz[16] and Newton,[17] they would have to say that every single one of them would have been viewed as the most untalented little fellows if they had been given these tests! The whole exercise would have been completely pointless. For Helmholtz, who is definitely regarded by those who design these tests as a great physicist, was hydrocephalic and was not at all gifted in his youth.

What is it that people are wanting to test? Merely the outer organism, simply what may be considered as man's physical instrument, the purely ahrimanic aspect of human nature! If the fruits of these ability tests are ever to have any significance for mankind, even more awful thought-forms will arise than those that have led to the present human catastrophe. The problem is that if one speaks to people today of what may perhaps lead to catastrophic events in a hundred years or so, this does not interest them. But we are living now in this transition from a luciferic educational system to an ahrimanic one, and we need to be among those who know how to understand such matters.

Human beings need to transform creative energies for the future into forces of the present; for this is what is demanded from us today—to confront the immediate reality of the present in an utterly true and unprejudiced way.

One can have some very strange experiences in doing this. I do not know whether I have already mentioned here an interesting experience of mine. Among the writings of Woodrow Wilson, there is one about freedom,[18] while another is just called *Literature*. These writings have been much admired and are still greatly admired by many. The one called *Literature* includes an interesting essay which Woodrow Wilson had written earlier about the historical development of America. There are also some other interesting essays by Woodrow Wilson that he had previously written on far-ranging aspects of history. When I read these writings I had an interesting experience. I found certain sentences which seemed remarkably familiar to me and which, nevertheless, had not been copied from anywhere; and yet they seemed remarkably familiar. And it very soon occurred to me that these sentences of Woodrow Wilson's could equally well have been written by Herman Grimm[19]— indeed, many of them can even be found word-for-word in Grimm. I love the work of Herman Grimm; as you well know, I do not exactly love Woodrow Wilson. Nevertheless, I cannot for that reason obscure the objective fact that with respect to the subject matter whole sentences of Herman Grimm's lectures and essays could simply have been taken from them and incorporated into Wilson's essays and, vice versa, sentences of Wilson's transposed into the works of Herman Grimm. As far as the simple wording of the text is concerned, these two people are saying exactly the same thing. But what we have to realize today is that when two people are saying the same thing, it is not the same! For the interesting fact is that Herman Grimm's sentences are personally fought for, he has struggled to formulate them painstakingly by degrees. Woodrow Wilson's very similar sounding sentences derive from a strange obsessiveness. The man is possessed by a subconscious ego that forces these sentences into conscious life.

Whoever is able to evaluate such things realizes that this is an instance of the general truth that whereas a grain of wheat is a grain of wheat, it makes a difference what kind of soil the grain of wheat is sown in. It makes a difference whether someone makes an idea his own by struggling for it bit by bit in his own, distinctly personal way, or whether one arrives at this idea by being possessed by the subconscious, with the result that everything rings forth from a possessed subconscious, from a consciousness that is possessed by the subconscious. Thus it is a question today of understanding that what matters is not the content of programmes but the living life that mankind lives.

One can teach materialistic philosophy, or the philosophy of mere ideas; one can teach a science that is purely materialistic, and it is possible to be an excellent European scholar by teaching such a science, a credit to the university and, moreover, a worthy citizen. There are quite a number of such people, I would say. They can be found everywhere, these ornaments and luminaries of science who are at the same time irreproachable, worthy citizens! This is indeed thoroughly possible. But take some particular idea, such as the struggle for existence (to mention a pretty commonplace idea), or an idea of the kind that more mild-mannered people like Oscar Hertwig[20] advocate, or ideas upheld by Spencer[21] and Mill[22] or Boutroux and Bergson,[23] who are certainly not aiming to penetrate to the spiritual domain but fail to go beyond a philosophy of mere ideas. But there is more to this than meets the eye; for if we take these ideas of materialistic science, it is true that they can flourish in the brains of good citizens, as I say; but whereas a grain of wheat is a grain of wheat, it makes a difference whether a grain of wheat is growing in fertile or stony ground, and it equally makes a difference whether the same scientific idea which can dawn on someone in Europe, brings credit to science and makes its mark at universities, has emerged from the brains of university lecturers or whether it derives from that of a person who has a brother who, while still a young man at the end of the 1880s, when he was a luminary of science in a laboratory in St Petersburg, a man who was richly imbued with ideas about chemistry and was honoured with a special medal by all those working with him (for he was highly respected while still a young man)—and then this brother suddenly disappears! He has been marked out by the university authorities, and suddenly he vanishes! In all manner of roundabout ways his colleagues are led to discover that he has meanwhile been hanged for taking part in the conspiracy against the reactionary Tsar Alexander III.[24] Such facts illumine current events like a flash of lightning. So it makes a difference whether the same idea lights up in the brain of a worthy West European university professor or in the brain of this man's brother who was hanged in such circumstances. When it enters the brain of this brother, it changes this brother into a Lenin[25] (for the brother of this person who was hanged was Lenin); and the same idea then becomes the driving force behind everything that you now see emerging in Eastern Europe.

An idea is an idea, just as a grain of wheat is a grain of wheat; but one must ask oneself whether an idea is the same if it arises in the brain of a university professor or in the brain of the brother of the man who was hanged. One must have the will to gaze into those depths of existence where lie the true impulses underlying events. Moreover, one must have the courage to reject the empty phrases of programmes and the ideas of scientists who believe that if they advocate something or other it will have a particular outcome. By means of a certain content one can advocate this or that idea; but what happens as a consequence depends on the relationship of this idea to a particular area of actual life, just as what happens to a grain of wheat depends on whether it falls in fertile or unfertile ground. It is necessary for mankind to seek in every sphere of life the path from abstraction, which in the present grave circumstances is everywhere leading to illusion or to chaos, to reality, which can be found only in a spiritual approach, a spiritual attitude. However long it may take, this is the only path whereby mankind can find healing and blessing amidst the confusion that prevails today.

This is what should be inscribed in our hearts, something in which we can feel united. This is something with which we should greet one another in earnest: that we share in this knowledge which has the potential to be the cure for mankind's afflictions. They can be healed, but one would in vain try to do so with quackery of any kind. They must be healed by something the lack of which has brought mankind into chaos.

Leninism would never have been able to take hold in the East if materialistic science, which sometimes does not even believe itself to be materialistic, had not been taught in the West. For what is done in the East is in an immediate sense a child of materialistic science. What emerged through Karl Marx[26] was a changeling. The true child of materialistic science already exists in the East. But one must have the will to acquire a real insight into these things.

This, my dear friends, is in a certain sense the background against which our building stands out. And the individual human beings working on this building think about it in a way that truly stands apart from the ideas that motivate people in so many countries today. One may well imagine that out there in other lands there are many people who consider that here human individuals are living who keep aloof from what preoccupies the world and, as these people believe, should indeed preoccupy it. It might be thought that people are viewing this place in a reproachful way. Those who have their hearts and souls in this building do not need to trouble themselves about such a reproach. For even if this building does not fulfil its task, even if this building does not achieve its purpose, what is working on this building and what is being achieved by those who are working with dedication on this building is something of the greatest importance in the present, something that has the potential to extricate mankind from its present predicament. And if people elsewhere believe that those working here are far removed from the tasks of humanity today, one must say to these people: here we are working on what is most important and most essential for the present, but these other people do not recognize this, they as yet know nothing of these things. But much will depend on mankind as a whole wanting to know something of what is happening here.

Once again let it be emphasized that the point is not whether this building achieves its purpose—although it would be good if it did so.

What matters is that the work on this building is being inspired by certain ideas that people have discovered for working on this building. Moreover, it is not the content of these ideas but the manner in which these ideas live that gives humanity impulses for the future, whereas the ideas that so many believe in today are essentially ideas of a former age which have a deathlike tendency and are ripe for the dissolution that now awaits them. We shall speak of this further tomorrow.

LECTURE 2

DORNACH, 18 AUGUST 1918

TODAY I should like to begin by making a kind of sketch of the human soul, as this human soul is in its relationship to the world and to itself. I should like to present this sketch in such a way that one can say: we are looking at a profile of man as a soul being. Thus in order that we may understand one another, it is as if we were to look at a physical human being—not the soul being—not in a full-face position but in profile and, shall we say, looking towards the right. Let us observe him thus.

Diagram 1

Of course, if we try to sketch something in this way we always have to bear in mind that we are dealing here with imaginative knowledge, and that therefore the essential reality lying behind such a phenomenon is being reproduced by means of a picture. The picture gives an indication of the phenomenon in question, and it is formed in such a way that it does so in a correct manner. But we should naturally not think of a drawing or sketch intended to represent something of a soul and spiritual nature in the way that one conceives of something which is a naturalistic copy of an outward, sense-perceptible reality. One has to be continually conscious of what I am now saying. So I shall omit everything relating to the physical and lower etheric body of man and shall try to sketch only the soul and soul-spiritual aspects [see Diagram 2].

As you know from various descriptions that I have given, this soul and spiritual aspect has a more direct connection with the world of soul and spirit than the physical human being has with his physical surroundings. The physical human being is to a significant degree separated off from his sense-perceptible environment. One could say that this physical, sense-perceptible human being is indeed enclosed within his skin. This is not so with the soul and spiritual aspect of man; for there one has to think in terms of a continual process of transition in the streams pulsating in his inner being of soul and spirit and in all the movements and currents flowing in the soul-spiritual world as a whole.

If I were to characterize from the one side the nature of the relationship of man's soul and spiritual being to the soul-spiritual aspect of his cosmic surroundings, I would perhaps have to do so in the following way. I would first have to paint what enters from the universe, from the infinitude of space, like this. I should really paint the whole space in this way, but this is not really necessary. I shall only paint what is in man's immediate environment. So this is what we may now understand as the surrounding world [see what is coloured blue in Diagram 2].

Now imagine in this pictorial form that soul-spiritual environment in which man is placed. Man is not yet there, of course; what is depicted by means of this blue colour is only what borders upon his domain from out of the surroundings. Imagine this to be like a surging blue sea that fills the surrounding space. (When I say 'blue sea', this must naturally be

Diagram 2

understood as I have often characterized it in the books that are available to you,[1] as colours are to be conceived of as a description of the aura, of the soul-spiritual domain.)

Another aspect of the world of soul and spirit now appears as it were floating or hovering, as though borne upwards like a wave. This is what I should have to describe now in the following way. Thus if we pass from the cosmic environment to man, we may think of ourselves and the soul-spiritual aspect of man as in a certain sense hovering in this red. There we would have one part of the soul-spiritual domain; and if we would make the sketch accord with reality we would have to render the upper part in a red that graduates into a kind of violet or lilac. This would be rightly shown only if the red was toned down to violet.

With this I have presented to you one pole of man's soul-spiritual nature. We arrive at the other pole if we order what relates in a floating or hovering way to the cosmic soul-spiritual surroundings by way of the physical human countenance somewhat as follows: yellow, green, orange; with green merging into the blue.

Here you have what I might call a normal human aura in profile, as seen from the right. I say explicitly a normal human aura in profile viewed from the right-hand side. That this figure has been shown to visionary perception as having this particular configuration characterizes the way that man is placed within his soul-spiritual environment. It also characterizes how man, as a being of soul and spirit, stands in relation to himself. If one studies what is portrayed by means of this figure, one can clearly see that man is a being who is bounded on two sides. These two sides which determine man's limited nature are always observed in life; but they are not interpreted correctly, they are not thought about in the right way and are, quite simply, not understood. You know that in ordinary scientific circles it is said that when man observes the world, when he wants to acquire knowledge of the world, he comes to definite limits in the knowledge that science can bequeath to him. We have often spoken of these limits, of this famous 'ignorabimus' (we shall never know),[2] the truth of which is asserted by scientists and many philosophers. It is said that man reaches certain limits in his knowledge, in his perception of the outer world. I have doubtless also mentioned to you the famous statement that Dubois-Reymond made at the Scientific Congress in Leipzig in the 1870s: human knowledge will never penetrate to the regions haunted by matter—this is roughly what Dubois-Reymond said at that time.[3]

A more appropriate way to speak about these limits of human knowledge would be to say that it is inevitable for man to formulate certain concepts in the course of his observation of the world which he encompasses neither with his scientific knowledge nor with his ordinary philosophical cognition. You need only to think of such phenomena as the concept of the atom. But the atom does of course only have meaning if one cannot speak of it, if one cannot say what an atom is; for the moment when one would begin describing the atom, it would no longer be an atom. There is something wholly unapproachable about it. Matter, actual substance itself, has a similar quality. Certain concepts have to be formulated, such as matter, force, and so on, to which one has no access.

The need for such concepts to be formulated simply rests on the fact that that soul-spiritual aspect of man which has an inwardly radiant quality is here extending into a dark void. What is stated to be the limit of knowledge can, I would say, actually be clearly seen in the aura. Man stands here before a boundary. His essential being is portrayed here in the aura by what I have allowed to flow from light green to blue-violet [see Diagram 2]. But by merging into blue-violet, it ceases to be man and becomes the encircling cosmos. Man's essential being, in which resides the inner power of his perception of the world, encounters a boundary or in a certain sense a nothingness, and he has to formulate concepts such as matter, atom, substance, force, which have no content. This resides in the way man's being is constituted, in his connection with the whole universe. Man's relationship with the universe is what is here unfolding. If we want to describe this boundary in accordance with the ideas of spiritual science, we can do so by saying that this boundary enables man with respect to his soul to come in contact with the universe. By indicating the direction towards the universe with one loop of a lemniscate, one can indicate what belongs to man with the other loop; although

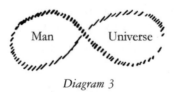

Diagram 3

what derives from man goes out into the universe. One therefore has to make the line of the loop, the lemniscate, open on one side and closed on the other, and draw it like this: here the line of the loop is closed, here it goes into infinity. It is the same line that I drew previously, except that here the two arms reach out to infinity.

Diagram 4

What I am drawing here as an open lemniscate, as an open loop, is not just something that has been thought out but something that you can indeed see as flashes streaming in and out in a gentle but very slow movement as an expression of man's relationship to the universe. The streaming movements of the universe continually approach man; he draws them towards him, they merge as they approach him and then stream out again. Thus something of this nature streams towards man, becomes intertwined and flows out again. He is permeated by these streaming movements originating from the universe which stop short in front of him. As you can imagine from this description, man is surrounded by a kind of wavelike aura; these streaming movements flow in from the universe, from a vortex and as it were greet man by forming a vortex in front of him, so that he is surrounded here by a kind of auric stream. This is essentially an expression of man's relationship to the universe, to his soul-spiritual surroundings.

You can find what you experience as lying in your consciousness depicted here as a mixture of blue, green and yellow, merging into orange towards the inner region. But at this point it comes up against something else; for within the inner region of man's soul being this yellow and orange encounters the soul-spiritual aspect of the lower part of man's being, which oscillates on the blue sea. What I have shown here as red merging into orange belongs to the subconscious parts of man and, indeed, also corresponds to those processes in the physical organism that are mainly involved with the activity of digestion and so forth, where consciousness plays no part. The region associated with consciousness would be characterized by the lighter parts of the aura as I have drawn them here [see Diagram 2]. Just as man's soul-spiritual

Diagram 5

nature is described here as meeting the soul-spiritual aspect of the surrounding world, so does it have an inner encounter with his subconscious, which indeed also forms part of the universe. I need to draw this meeting of the streams in such a way that one of them reaches out to infinity; whereas I have to draw the encounter within man in a different way. Here I must also draw a loop, but I have to draw this one so that it has an inward orientation. Please notice that I am still drawing a loop, but I am taking the lower loop and inverting it, so that it goes like this:

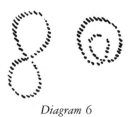

Diagram 6

So I invert the lower loop [see drawing, on the right]. In contrast to the above Diagram 5, where I cause one of the loops to open out to infinity, I now invert the lower loop. With this, I have given a pictorial image of the obstacles that arise when the inner aspect of the soul-spiritual domain makes contact with the subconscious—and, hence, also cosmic—soul and spiritual world. I must therefore characterize these obstacles that arise in man, if I draw them in a manner that corresponds to them, in this way [seven lemniscates with inverted loops]. These are the obstacles that correspond to an inner wave or undulation within man [Diagram 7].

If you trace the course of this inner wave, its main direction—and only its main direction—runs along beside the junction of those nerves which are, as you know, incorrectly referred to as the sensory and motor nerves. This is only said in passing, for my wish today is to concentrate on describing the soul-spiritual aspect of this phenomenon.

Diagram 7

With this you can see the strong contrast that exists in man's relationship to his soul-spiritual surroundings and to himself, namely to that portion that he absorbs from these surroundings as his subconscious and which I have had to sketch here as the red wave floating on the universal blue sea of the soul-spiritual cosmos.

We have said that this wave here [see Diagram 2 on the right] corresponds in a certain sense to the barrier that man comes up against if he wants to know about the outer world. But here too [on the left of the same diagram] there is a barrier; there is a barrier within man himself. Were this barrier not present, you would be perpetually looking at your inner being. Everyone would be looking within himself. So just as if this barrier [on the right] were not there man would behold the outer world, he would in the same way gaze into his inner being if this barrier [the one on the left] did not exist. It is indeed the case that if a person were to look into himself in the present cycle of evolution he would derive little joy from doing so, because what he would see is a thoroughly imperfect, chaotic seething turbulence in his inner nature, something that could give no great pleasure; but it is what mystics who are divorced from reality believe they can perceive when they speak of mysticism. What is very often regarded by these mystics as a goal worthy of their aspirations, especially any such mystics—whom I characterized on a previous occasion last year[4]—who really believe that when they look into themselves they are able to learn about the universe in accordance with their mystic path, all this is veiled, wholly concealed, by this blockage. Man cannot look into himself. What is formed within this region [left] is dammed up and is reflected, for it can at least be reflected; and this reflective quality is manifested in memory, our faculty of recollection. Every time a thought or an impression that you have apprehended is recollected in memory, it does so through the working of this wave of obstruction. If you did not have this inner barrier, every impression that you receive from outside, every thought that you grasp, would pass through you, would be unable to remain within you and would go out into the rest of the soul-spiritual universe. You retain the impressions that you receive only because you have this inner wave of obstruction. Because of this, however, you are in a position to recall your impressions through certain processes still to be described; and this comes to expression in the functioning of recollection, of memory. Thus you can picture to yourself that you have within you something like a flat surface, which is drawn here [in the diagram] in profile (for this is how it is drawn; there is such a plane within you), where what is not supposed to penetrate is thrust back. When you are awake you remain united with the outside world, otherwise in the waking state everything would go through you. You would actually know nothing of impressions; you would receive impressions but would be unable to hold on to them.

This is what is signified by memory. And the obstructive surface that gives rise to our memory conceals what mystics who are divorced from reality would very much like to behold within themselves. As for what is in these nether regions, it could be said that anyone who really knows about these things would cherish the saying that man 'should never wish to behold what they [the Gods] have mercifully concealed with night and obscurity'.[5] But mystics live in their fantasies and want to behold these inner regions. However, they are unable to do so in any case, because they would undermine and corrupt normal consciousness to such an extent that the wave of recollection would not be thrust back. That same quality that constitutes our memory, which is so necessary to us for outward life, is what conceals all that these mystics would like to see but which man is not supposed to look upon. Underlying your memory, what causes your memory and what lies at its surface is an essential aspect of man. But just as the back, or coating, of a mirror reflects back what is in front of it, what is in your consciousness does not pass behind it; it is thrown back and is therefore able to continue there as memory. Thus our whole life can be reflected as a memory. What we call the life of our ego is essentially the reflecting of this memory.

So you see that our conscious life is actually lived between this wave on the right and this one on the left. We would therefore be like sieves that let everything through if we did not have this wave of obstruction which is the basis for memory; and we would have insight into mysteries beyond the limits of knowledge if we were not obliged to form concepts for what is outside the sense-perceptible realm, for which we have no content. If we were organized in such a way that we were unable to produce this wave of obstruction, we would be like sieves. If we were organized so that we did not need to formulate these dark concepts devoid of content, we would be loveless beings incapable of love, and with stony and barren hearts. Nothing in the world would please us, we would all have a similar nature to Mephistopheles.

It is because we are organized in such a way that we are unable to approach the soul-spiritual aspect of our environment with our abstract concepts, with our intellectual capacities, that we are able to love. For it would not be right for us to approach what we should love by analysing it in the ordinary sense of the word, by dissecting it and treating it as chemists treat chemical substances in the laboratory. We do not love when we engage in chemical analysis or synthesis. The faculty of memory and the capacity for love are two qualities which correspond at one and the same time to two boundaries of human nature. The faculty of memory corresponds to the inner boundary; what lies beyond the zone of memory is the inner realm of man's subconscious. The other zone corresponds to the power of love; and what lies beyond this zone corresponds to the soul-spiritual aspect of the universe. Thus the unconscious part of human nature lies beyond the one zone, in so far as man's inner realm extends; whereas the soul-spiritual aspect of the universe reaches without limit into the expanses lying beyond the other zone.

We can therefore speak of the zone of love and the zone of memory, and man's soul-spiritual being can be encompassed within these zones; but beyond the one zone [see Diagram 2, left-hand side] we must seek what remains unconscious—and remains so for the reason that it is very strongly connected with the bodily nature of man, with his bodily organism. Naturally things are in reality not as simple as they have to be portrayed, because everything is interwoven with everything else. What is drawn here in red [see Diagram 2] extends into other areas and is changed; and what is green and blue is also subject to change. Everything actually merges into everything else. Nevertheless, for the most part the drawing that has been sketched is correct and corresponds to the facts.

But from this you can see that physical life here on Earth has a strong and conscious spiritual aspect to it. Here [left] is an unconscious spiritual domain which merges into the universe. These two parts of man's being can be very closely distinguished from one another. This spiritual region in the middle is specifically for earthly life, and therefore very subtly woven. Everything here [yellow] is what I might call finely woven light. If I had to show where this finely woven light is in man, I would have to go to what I have been so minutely describing—the human head. What I have thus described, what I have drawn over on the other side in yellow, yellow-green and yellow-orange is what might be called finely woven spirit-light. This has no strong affinity with earthly matter; it actually has the least possible connection with earthly matter. Because it has little affinity it is also difficult for it to form a connection with matter, and so it remains for the greater part unconnected with it (and the matter that is made available to this part actually derives from a person's previous incarnation). The head, that which forms the human head, the formative forces of the human head, are essentially drawn from the previous incarnation; and there is but a loose connection between this delicately woven soul-spiritual nature and the bodily nature, which is actually held together out of the previous incarnation. The qualities and capacities of your physiognomy are carried over from your previous incarnation. Those who know about understanding people gain insight through the physiognomy of the head—not through what derives from an inner luciferic source but, rather, through the manner in which a person adapts himself to the outer universe. One has to look at the physiognomy as though it were impressed into a person: it is not so much that it is the result of this process, but one must in a certain sense regard it as the negative counter-picture of the soul realm; it is this that one sees in this negative image of the face. If you were to form an impression of any face you would actually see a physiognomy that betrays to an extreme degree what you did in your previous incarnation. On the other hand, everything that I have sketched in those nether regions as being connected only with the surging sea of the soul-spiritual aspect of the world, all that is to be conceived as corresponding to man's subconscious or unconscious, is strongly related to the bodily nature and fully pervades it. This bodily nature is connected with the spiritual domain in such a way that the latter is barely able to manifest itself in its own right. Hence if one were to look down at this region one would perceive this intermingling of the spiritual and bodily aspects that lies beyond the threshold of memory. This is what prepares the head of the next incarnation and seeks to be metamorphosed into what will acquire solid material form only in the future and will become head only in the next incarnation. For man's head has become overdeveloped, with the result that its development—as you may recall from previous lectures that I have given here—has actually come to an end by a person's twenty-seventh or twenty-eighth year. In the form of the head there is already an overdevelopment of man.

But strange as it may seem, the rest of man is also a head; although his development in this respect has not yet approached that of the head itself. If you imagine a person who has been beheaded, what remains is also a human head but at a greatly retarded stage. If it develops further it will also become a head, whereas what you have as the human head has been the rest of the organism in a previous incarnation. If you think of what in your present organism is not yet head as disembodied, freed from the body, thus if you think the head away from your present organism which will become a head only in the next incarnation (even though this organism of yours is but an image, everything physical is an image of something spiritual), if you imagine instead the spiritual aspect of what in its outward form has not yet appeared in man, you see this manifested in our luciferic figure of the Group,[6] this is what you are seeing!

And now imagine all that is of a soul-spiritual nature which has been held back from your head, thus all that represents a barrier for man and which he cannot penetrate [see Diagram 2, on the right], compressed into the human head; then man will not have the old, dignified head that he ordinarily possesses but he will have a fossilized-looking head, as bony as the figure of Ahriman in our Group.

Thus if you imagine what lies beneath the boundary of memory spread throughout man's inner being, you arrive at all that is luciferic; and if you think of everything that is beyond this wave of obstruction [on the right of Diagram 2] extended into the human figure, you get the ahrimanic form. And man is between the two.

What I have been explaining to you here has considerable significance—not only for an understanding of man but also for an understanding of the spiritual processes at work in human evolution. Unless we have a fundamental understanding of these things we shall never be able to understand how Christianity and the Christ impulse have entered the evolution of mankind. It is also impossible to understand the part that the Catholic Church has played, the roles of Jesuitism and similar streams and those of the East and West if one does not view them in connection with these matters.

I shall allow myself to say something to you tomorrow about these streams, such as those of East and West, Jesuitism, Americanism and so on, which can be properly understood only if one has a clear awareness of what lies at the foundation of man's soul-spiritual being.

LECTURE 3

YESTERDAY I tried to give you a picture of the soul being of man. What we particularly want to take from this picture of man as a soul being today are the two boundary zones that we learnt about yesterday. The one boundary zone comes about as a result of man's need to come to a halt when he tries to penetrate the outer world as it appears to his senses. Scientists, philosophers and others speak of the limits to knowledge. We know that these limits to knowledge do not really exist, that they are actually only a reality for man's physical sense-perception.

The other boundary is the result of everything existing in or entering our consciousness being in a certain sense reflected back, mirrored back at an inner threshold and thereby enabled to become memory. What we have in our consciousness does not enter right into the depths of that region of which man has no more than a subconscious awareness. We shall draw these two boundaries [see diagram]: the boundary of memory [left], and what we can really call the boundary of the capacity for love [right], which is at the same time the limit of our knowledge of nature. We indicated these earlier by here [right] drawing lemniscates that are open to the outside and here [left] drawing lemniscates of a different kind with an inverted loop. So this one [on the right] is the outer region which man can no longer perceive with his ordinary powers of sense-perception and is, therefore, imperceptible. This one [on the left] is the inner boundary of conscious life, which man is unable to penetrate with his consciousness. He remains with his consciousness above this boundary. Were he to dive down there with his conscious ideas, he would have no memory.

Diagram 1

Now in connection with man's soul existence there is something quite definite that can be said in the light of these two boundaries. If we go back in human evolution somewhat beyond the eighth century BC (you will recall that the fourth post-Atlantean epoch began in 747 BC), if we go back beyond this period into the earlier post-Atlantean epochs, what lies beyond this boundary [on the right] still in a certain way exerted an influence upon man's consciousness. The atavistic clairvoyance that still existed at that time was indeed dependent on this. Certain impulses from the cosmos were flowing in at that time, and these made themselves manifest as atavistic visionary powers. Hence we can say that this outer domain has become impenetrable—I mean intellectually impenetrable—only since the eighth century BC, and it has become ever more and more impenetrable. We are living now in the fifth post-Atlantean epoch, and it is now thoroughly impenetrable. People today have become inordinately insistent about this, constantly maintaining that no one is able to penetrate to that 'thing in itself' (as they call it) that lies beyond this boundary.

On the other hand it should be said that another tendency is increasingly making itself felt, and as we approach the sixth post-Atlantean epoch this will be ever more the case. This is that this zone here [left] will in a certain sense become penetrable. The time will come when from the depths of human nature, a region which I described to you yesterday as an intermingling of spiritual and bodily aspects and which man should not endeavour to behold (at any rate, not in the way that mystics who are divorced from reality would wish), all manner of things will want to seep through from the sixth post-Atlantean epoch onwards. Yes, this time will begin already in the fifth post-Atlantean epoch, in our own epoch. All kinds of things will want to leak through. This will show itself above all in that far more people than one would think today will deduce from purely inner experiences that there are repeated earthly lives, for example. Even today, albeit not very often, such insights are beginning to break through. I have frequently mentioned[1]—here, among other places[2]—of a remarkable man of our present time, Otto Weininger,[3] who is known especially for his thick book *Geschlecht und Charakter* ('Race and Character'). Of even greater interest, however, is that book of his which his friend Rappaport published after his death, where there are all sorts of interesting things. It consists for the most part of aphorisms. The volume bears the title *Über die letzten Dinge* ('Concerning Last Things'). One of these aphorisms[4] says something along these lines: Weininger maintains that the human soul may have developed a certain dread of itself in its life before birth and because of this has acquired the longing to forget this life and bury itself in forgetfulness, and this is the significance of the process of incarnating. Thus Weininger unreservedly speaks about the life before birth, about the process of incarnating; but he speaks in a gloomy, pessimistic way of how the soul seeks to blot out all memory of its life before birth, and tries to achieve this by incarnating in a physical human body.

There are many examples of people today who have such direct impressions of the path of the soul, and they will become increasingly numerous. It is possible to see today in a person such as Weininger how the ego is inwardly taking hold of man in what I might call a more solid and compact way. One clearly sees in Weininger's case how this boundary is becoming more permeable and how all manner of things are rising up from there. It is, for example, interesting to read the notes which he wrote about his own death. When he was still only 23 years old, he committed suicide. He wrote a whole series of notes which are extraordinarily interesting, because they are exact portrayals of imaginations of astral perception. This was coupled with a certain trait of character which led him one day to rent the house where Beethoven had died in Vienna and then to kill himself there the following morning at the age of 23. And the theme of what he had noted down was that he would have to kill himself, because he would otherwise be in dread of being forced by an undefined urge to become a murderer, to have to murder someone else.[5]

One can see how the most terrible things are here wreaking havoc in the soul of an extraordinarily gifted man which cannot be so easily overcome by what is in his consciousness, because there is so much rising up from his subconscious. You will understand that there is a certain justification in indicating that the ordinary cleverness that man is now able to develop is not sufficient in order to know what is welling up from these unknown depths. For it should not be emerging in this way, it should remain below; but it will nevertheless do so. Just as until the year 747 BC something entered in from without, henceforth something will rise up from within; and this cannot by any means whatsoever be mastered by the cleverness that man will normally be able to achieve. What is needed here is the understanding of the world that can be acquired through spiritual science. It is possible for harmony, inner steadfastness and inner solidity to permeate man's life of soul only when people begin to want to bring order and harmony to this inner soul life through what can be acquired from knowledge of the spirit. Human evolution is therefore reaching forward from a state where the outer world was more perceptible than it is today to one where more will emerge from man's innermost depths than is normally the case today.

The things of which I am now speaking are thoroughly familiar to circles of initiates. The whole of Eastern esoteric life, the whole life of the spirit in Asia, continues even now to reflect that ancient knowledge that was accessible to human beings until the eighth century BC. Indeed, not only esoteric life but also the whole of Asiatic culture. This is why it is so difficult for a European to understand when an Oriental, someone from Asia, speaks about his culture. In order to understand these people one needs to arrive at a different way of forming thoughts and ideas. For example, it should be of the greatest interest to a large number of people today to study something as characteristic as the address that the Indian Rabindranath Tagore,[6] gave about the spirit of Japan. You will be aware that Tagore is the Indian author who has been awarded the Nobel Prize for Literature. He gave a lecture about the spirit of Japan. What he said about this theme is of less importance than the spirit out of which he was speaking, namely that of the modern Oriental, which can be understood only if one knows that in the Oriental something still remains of that in-streaming, dawning light of the outer world which is no longer perceptible today. For most Europeans, what Orientals say when they are speaking in a way that is in tune with their culture is virtually unintelligible. Generally speaking, it is impossible to understand what they are talking about.

And then there is this other phenomenon, that what should really only be appearing in the future is being anticipated. I might compare this with children who as children already have the characteristics of old age; they take on these qualities when they are still only children. An irregularity enters into evolution when something that ought to come later is thrust forward into an earlier time. Whereas in oriental thinking, in the oriental way of looking at the world, there is especially in the most outstanding spirits something that is left over from an ancient past in the manner that I have indicated, in individuals who think so completely in accordance with Americanism something is introduced or thrust forward which belongs to a later time. If one is able to enter into such things, one can clearly see that such individual spirits have within them much of what seeps through here [left]. You get an idea of what is thus seeping through if, for example, you read the essay[7] that Woodrow Wilson has written about the development of the American people, and in particular the North American people. One cannot imagine anything that more hits the nail on the head and is more apt than this essay that Woodrow Wilson has written about the development of the American people. Every word of it gives one the feeling that the whole matter is characterized and dealt with in the shrewdest possible way. And this is particularly striking because in this case Wilson very sharply emphasizes that a large number of people even in America hold a view that is justified only if one considers the American people as still representing a dependency of the English people—a view that he, Woodrow Wilson, contests. Woodrow Wilson is in the fullest sense of the word opposed to those people who still today look upon Americans as if they were descendants, or a particular category, of English people originating in Europe; and he considers that they understand nothing of the actual development of the American people in the nineteenth century. For— and here Wilson is speaking out of a quintessentially American spirit, with great precision and aptness—Americans only begin inwardly to be Americans at the moment when they cease to be connected in their souls with what came from England, when they start blazing their trail from East to West, from the East coast of America to the West coast. In this trekking through the primeval forests, in the work with shotgun and spade, with horse and plough, in this overcoming of those obstacles in the course of forging the way from East to West, there developed what he calls the man of the West, the 'Western man'. In a manner that makes a direct and highly convincing impression, he describes this way of conquering the ground as the real pulse of American development. In all this one has the feeling—for in such a case one must of course learn to discern the 'how' and not merely the 'what'—that there is far more standing behind these words than Wilson alone. For when Wilson himself speaks, there's nothing very clever about what he says. What stands behind his words are demonic beings who possess his inner nature, imparting future mysteries of immense magnitude. Mankind would need to penetrate these secrets if evolution is to be understood.

It is necessary to make a distinction between the purely scientific and journalistic understanding of the world—one that requires no particular effort and is all too popular—and a true understanding of the world. This true understanding of the world must be able to recognize such contrasting things as I have been discussing here: on the one hand the capacity of oriental people to be receptive to something coming from without [see diagram, on the right] and, on the other, the emergence in Americans of something that lies within [left]. What emerges in them is not necessarily to be dismissed out of hand; in a certain sense it can be construed as a majestic ahrimanic revelation. For these excellent remarks by Woodrow Wilson about the development of the American people essentially represent an ahrimanic revelation.

The initiates of the East and the initiates of the American people know what it is necessary to make of these things. There is an impulse on the part of each to guide the evolution of mankind into certain channels. The oriental peoples—or rather their initiates—have quite particular intentions for the future evolution of mankind. These people see what the right path of evolution is and try to influence it (to the extent that they are able). They try to give it a certain direction, a certain impulse. And the impulse that the oriental initiates want to give to evolution is essentially that one should no longer reckon on their being any human generation after approximately the first half of the sixth post-Atlantean epoch. One would give up on the idea of the earthly human race after this time. Human evolution would be brought to the point where human beings do not really any longer have physical descendants and where souls are spiritualized, so that they cease to descend to Earth in bodily incarnations. From the middle of the sixth post-Atlantean epoch the intention would be to establish for humanity the kingdom of the spirit. This would only be possible if one were to reject certain elements of culture. It is not only the initiates of the East who have a distinctly negative attitude towards certain European characteristics but every cultured Oriental actually shares this aversion instinctively; and they reject precisely those characteristics of which Europeans are particularly proud. Thus they have no use for everything that has resulted from the purely technical, material culture in Europe and in its American offshoot.

Anyone who studies human evolution, particularly in the nineteenth century and on into the twentieth century, will find that there is jus-tification in saying that technology has made very considerable progress in depriving man of his capacity to work.[8] When it is said that the Earth has so many hundred million inhabitants, this is not really quite correct; because one can also reckon how many inhabitants the Earth has according to how much work is done. However, it would be perfectly justifiable to say that since the last third of the eighteenth century human labour has been carried out by the machines that have gradually been produced. One can gauge—and fairly precisely—how many millions of additional people the Earth would have to have if all the work that is undertaken by machines were to be carried out by human beings. The Earth would need to have five hundred million extra people. It can indeed be said that there are on the Earth not only those people who have two legs and a head and who can be statistically counted, but five hundred million more people, if measured according to work capacity; but the labour is being performed by machines.

However, there is nothing material that does not have a spiritual dimension in the background. These five hundred million human forces represent an opportunity for the equivalent number of ahrimanic demons to take up their abode in human culture. These ahrimanic demons are indeed present; and oriental people strongly repudiate these ahrimanic demons out of a certain instinct—they don't like them at all. You see this in every case of a highly cultured Oriental; he rejects this ahrimanic demonology. For this ahrimanic demonology gives people a certain heaviness, which rules out the possibility of any fulfilment of the aim of oriental initiation, namely that by the middle of the sixth post-Atlantean epoch the human race will physically cease to exist on the Earth. Human beings will be held back by what is being developed in this demonically ahrimanic way.

The initiates of Americanism have a different aim in view. Indeed, their goal is a completely opposite one. Their endeavour is to form a more intimate bond than is normally the case in human evolution between human souls and that bodily nature that will be found on Earth, the dense, coarse physicality that will come to exist on Earth from the sixth post-Atlantean epoch onwards. The soul culture will be greatly intensified, but the bodily aspect will be coarse. In the American West the aim will be to cultivate a closer connection with this coarse physicality than is normally the case, a deeper penetration into one's bodily nature. There will be a reaching towards what is seeping through [see diagram, left], brought about by a deeper immersion in the body. Whereas Orientals want to establish a culture where human bodies have no place in the future evolution of the Earth, the aim of the American culture of the West is to chain human souls to this subsequent earthly evolution. To the extent that this can be achieved, bodies will be formed in such a way that once souls have passed through death they will be able to descend once more as quickly as possible into a body and spend the minimum amount of time in the spiritual world. Human souls will be held back as much as possible from residing for any length of time in the spiritual world; the aim is that they return to the Earth as rapidly as they can, that they are intimately connected with earthly life.

These are tendencies that one must recognize. However strange it may appear to people today to speak of these tendencies, it will be harmful to them if they are overlooked. For it is necessary that they enter with full consciousness into what is required of them, with regard to which they unfortunately often behave in such a way as to justify the remark that they simply allow things to take their course.

However, this Western ideal, this tendency to allow demons to hold sway over man, can be attained only if the soul-spiritual aspect of Americanism can be supported by another stream or world conception that is far more closely connected with Americanism than one might think. As you have seen, the most striking feature of Americanism is its inclination towards an ahrimanic culture. But this aspect of American culture would receive a considerable stimulus from another world conception which is far more closely related to it than one might suppose. This is Jesuitism. Jesuitism and Americanism are two phenomena which have much to do with one another. For at the beginning of the fifth post-Atlantean epoch it was a question of finding an impulse through which a situation could be created where people were led as far as possible from an understanding of Christ; and the cultural impulse that set itself the task of bringing this about, of completely undermining all understanding of Christ, is Jesuitism. The aim of Jesuitism is gradually to eradicate any possibility of understanding the Christ; for what lies at its foundation is associated with a deep mystery. Man's capacity to receive something from without [see diagram, right] into his inner being has always been associated, as I have said, with the atavistic clairvoyance that human beings had prior to the seventh and eighth centuries of the pre-Christian era. Moreover, as a result of this atavistic clairvoyance they also beheld Christ in the cosmos. The Christ was an object of their perception in the old clairvoyance. I have often pointed this out; I described it in *Occult Science*,[9] and the whole meaning of my book *Christianity as Mystical Fact*[10] ultimately culminates in this idea. Christ was seen in the cosmos, Christ was seen in the universe. But now consider this: from the seventh and eighth pre-Christian centuries human beings have lost the possibility of beholding the universe. What, then, would people have lost—if nothing else had happened—through being unable any longer to look out into the universe? What would they have lost? They would have lost the possibility of knowing anything at all about a Christ spirit had the Christ not come down to the Earth. At the historical moment of time when human beings were no longer able to perceive Christ in the cosmos, Christ came down to the Earth and united Himself with Jesus. From then on it has been man's task to understand how Christ dwells within him; and some way needs to be found of ensuring that, together with what is seeping through here [see the left of the diagram], the Christ is recognized. For Christ has descended to mankind. Jesus is a human being in whom the Christ has dwelt. True human self-knowledge must be the bearer of the germinal impulse of Jesus, so that it will be possible to move on into the future. It is deeply significant that we speak of a Christ Jesus. For Christ corresponds to the cosmic aspect; but this cosmic element has come down to the Earth and has taken up His abode in Jesus, and Jesus corresponds to the earthly realm together with the entire future of the Earth.

If there is an endeavour to sever man's connection with the spiritual world, he will also lose his connection with Christ. The possibility then arises to make use of Jesus in such a way that the Earth continues to exist only in its earthly aspect. You will therefore find in Jesuitism a continual battle against Christology and, indeed, a strong emphasis on there being an army for Jesus. It is not surprising that spiritual science should be a means for making these things known, for causing the scales to fall from people's eyes. Hence those who do not want to be recognized will become increasingly angry about the aims of spiritual science. And the fury grows: the July issue of the Jesuit journal *Stimmen der Zeit* ('Voices of the Time')—formerly *Stimmen aus Maria-Laach*—contains not only one but two articles against me.[11] And anyone who can link this with new Jesuit aspirations that are developing elsewhere in the world will be able to see something deeper in all this. Unfortunately, however, one speaks of these things mostly to people who are asleep.

People love to sleep through the most important things and to fail to listen to what is actually determining the future. As I said the day before yesterday, everything will come upon people as a surprise. They even want to be surprised. If one speaks at the earliest possible moment about things that are of crucial relevance to the time, people regard this as upsetting; for as worthy members of the bourgeoisie they would rather sit comfortably in their armchairs for as long as possible, even if they hold responsible, leading positions in society. But those who are interested in spiritual science should have it engraved in their souls that everything will be done to make spiritual science ineffective. Above all, it is not exactly a good thing when even we in our circles are only too inclined to sleep where what is going on in the world is concerned.

Sometimes it is hard to see that all the personal goings-on are given a higher place than what is of such particular importance and significance in our present time, namely attending to the great concerns of humanity as they are gradually unfolding. The attacks which have to do with powerful will-impulses come from a great variety of sources of opposition, which need to be taken seriously. Such an attack as the one to which I have referred must in a certain sense be taken more seriously. One has to be able to assess it in the right way. Less serious attention should be given to those snide attacks that constantly well up from the subterranean regions of our society, and which to some extent have an evil aspect merely because again and again one can observe the tendency for there to be the greatest and most ardent sympathy for those people who malign and seek to denigrate what is striven for in our circles. Only when the harm has been done do people gradually decide to look properly for themselves; but up to now many people have been lionized who have gone on to do damage.

I say this not because I think that one thing or another should be different but because I feel obliged to draw attention to the need for humanity to wake up and to the great importance of our being among those who are striving for the truth.

In certain spheres today more or less anything can be achieved. But the sleep of humanity to which I have referred, which can be overcome only by gaining insight into the spiritual worlds, is extraordinarily difficult to overcome. And with respect to the dissemination of spiritual-scientific knowledge one has to wrestle even more with this sleep than with opponents. I am not referring to any particular instance of this, but in our whole cultural environment there is something sleepy about the very impulses that are sprouting everywhere from people's heads. Two things need to be engraved in one's soul today like golden rules. Never has there been such a need as in our fifth post-Atlantean epoch for people to make an increasing effort—which I do not doubt that they can succeed in doing—to achieve what is of such particular value: understanding spiritual-scientific knowledge. It is true that spiritual-scientific knowledge has to be sought through clairvoyant insight into the spiritual world; that is a necessity. It goes without saying that there must be clairvoyants to research into the spiritual world, that there must be those who strive for spiritual knowledge. Secondly, however, it is of particular importance that people are found who are by virtue of their intellectual power able to understand this spiritual-scientific knowledge, this knowledge that has been sought in supersensible worlds. The rational grasp of spiritual science is vitally necessary today, for it is the means whereby the opposing cultural forces are overcome. Man's intellect today is so vast that the whole of spiritual science can be understood where there is a will. Moreover, cultivating an understanding of this nature is a matter of universal cultural interest and not an egotistical affair. For such an understanding can be striven for if those intellectual forces which are employed today in scientific domains on all sorts of trivial projects, frittered away in modern economic life and, moreover, applied in a futile and perhaps even soul-destroying technology are to be used in a suitable way, so that people are no longer misguided from their earliest childhood onwards. One would then see how easily the treasures of spiritual knowledge could indeed be channelled towards an understanding of humanity. This is the one aspect.

The other golden rule is this, that something more is needed today if the gifts of the spirit are to be made fruitful for our culture. The first is something that must be wrested from Ahriman. People today are so clever, for Ahriman sees to it that this is so. Oh, how clever people are! But they apply their cleverness only for materialistic ends. People are not merely clever, they are super-clever. We shall speak of this further in the coming lectures, in order that you may see what an immense influence the ahrimanic element has on the super-cleverness of modern times. But something else is also necessary. Much still needs to be wrested from another spirit. We need not merely cleverness with which to gain a real insight into spiritual knowledge but we need above all and with the greatest urgency—the words are barely adequate—qualities of liveliness, enthusiasm, fire and warmth in those human souls who are the recipients of these spiritual gifts. We need people who can demonstrate the reality of these spiritual riches with the whole of their souls. It is in the realm of the inner life that this knowledge must be wrested from the luciferic powers, which are now so active in the world. There is a beautiful vista: it is the picture of someone who in calm clarity, but with an inner fire and enthusiasm because it is for him a necessity, is able to engender an inner warmth for this spiritual knowledge. But there is another picture, that of someone who tries to lull himself to sleep by means of this spiritual knowledge, to become dreamy and imbued with warmth, to expand into the forces of the universe and unite his soul with the divine all. These are contrasts that can easily be observed at the present time, contrasts which it is necessary to observe. For it will not be easy to incorporate what we receive from the spirit into human culture; and yet this must be done, human culture needs it. People will not only have to learn to think very differently, they will also have to feel and experience things in a different way.

Well, I could say a lot more about what I have just said, but I would prefer to stop now so that you have the opportunity to think about it. There is much food for thought in what has been aroused by deceitfulness of various kinds, which I have deliberately included in the substance of what I have presented. We shall continue to speak of these things when next we meet.

LECTURE 4

I<small>F</small> one wants to understand the age in which one is living, one needs to understand it in a wider cosmic context. The limitation of the present age is that people do not want to understand the forces and impulses at work in our time from a wider perspective; and in order to gain any clarity about what is going on today it will be increasingly necessary to recall the circumstances surrounding human evolution at the time of the Mystery of Golgotha. We have considered the Mystery of Golgotha from the most varied points of view and have seen how deeply and with what significance it has entered into the whole evolutionary process, the whole evolution of humanity. We know that human beings experienced and perceived the world differently before the Mystery of Golgotha from the way they did afterwards. Of course, there was not an immediate transition from one condition to the other. But if we look back over this time we see the appropriateness of what we have explained from a number of different points of view. In order to form a foundation for what I shall go on to say, I should like to refer to one thing in particular.

If we consider the mood and state of mind of people before the Mystery of Golgotha, we can make the general observation that amongst the more cultured part of mankind, those people from whom our present cultural life has emerged, there was before the Mystery of Golgotha a certain faculty of beholding the mysteries of the spiritual cosmos. It goes without saying that before the Mystery of Golgotha people did not look up at the starry heavens in the way one does today.

We know very well that when someone looks up at the stars today he says to himself: other planets are connected with our Earth which orbit together with it around the Sun, and then there are countless other fixed stars which likewise have their planets. And if people then pay heed to the kind of thoughts that they are having when they reflect in this way, they will have to admit that their idea is one of a vast cosmic mechanism. That anything else is having any effect or influence beyond the forces of this vast cosmic mechanism is only very, very dimly recognized; whereas for people living before the Mystery of Golgotha this was more or less self-evident. They especially took it for granted that the Sun, for example, is not merely the sort of object that the modern physicist perceives, that is, roughly speaking, a kind of fiery ball out there in space, but that this Sun of which physics speaks is only *one* element of the whole Sun. For the Sun has a soul and spiritual foundation; and the spiritual essence underlying the Sun was referred to by the Greek sage[1] as the universal goodness of the world, the goodness of the cosmos, a goodness that swirls through and unifies the world. This was to him the spirit of the Sun. To this Greek sage it would have seemed to be a monstrous superstition to think, as does the modern physicist, that there is nothing but a fiery ball out there in space. To him this fiery ball hovering in space was the manifestation of a unifying goodness which has a central part to play in the world. And linked to this spiritual goodness, which has so central a role, there is also a soul aspect, which the Greeks called Helios. The physical Sun was merely the third element in the sequence, the physical expression of the good and of Helios. Thus people of that time saw in the place occupied by the Sun something of a threefold nature. And the people whose minds were active at the time of the Mystery of Golgotha, individuals who, as sages, were furnished with a knowledge of this Mystery of Golgotha and of the ancient mysteries, united this threefold mystery that was perceived in the Sun in former times with the Christ mystery, with the Mystery of Golgotha itself. For those with the requisite knowledge, veneration of the Sun was associated with veneration of Christ; for them, Sun wisdom was deeply connected with Christ wisdom.

In order to feel what I have been characterizing here as part of one's natural experience of the world, it was necessary for there to have been the soul constitution particular to that time. But this constitution of soul was even then disappearing. It had already been disappearing since the eighth century before Christ, beginning from the year 747 BC, the actual date of the founding of Rome. At the time of the founding of Rome the possibility that had formerly existed of perceiving the spiritual world out in the cosmos was vanishing; and when Rome entered the arena of history what we may call a prosaic element became part of human evolution. The Greeks, for example, preserved in the whole of their world conception the possibility of seeing behind the Sun the other two Suns, its soul and its spirit; and it was only because the Mystery of Golgotha did not occur in the world of Greek wisdom and Greek sensibilities but, rather, in that of Roman wisdom and Roman sensibilities that it came about that the link with the knowledge of Christ's connection with the spiritual Sun was severed. Especially the Church Fathers and Christian teachers have sought to enshroud the mystery of the Sun, to cause this mystery of the Sun to be forgotten by mankind, to prevent it from becoming known. Throughout the subsequent development of Christianity (as it is called), a veil was destined to be spread over the deeply meaningful and all-encompassing wisdom of Christ's connection with the mystery of the Sun.

If one were to define the task of the Church, the Church that owed its origin to Christianity having entered into the cultural domain of Rome, one would have to say that the Christian Church, coloured as it was by Rome, had the particular task of enshrouding the Christ mystery to the greatest possible degree and of ensuring that it was as little known as possible. The kind of institution that the Church became in its Roman context was particularly suited to letting people know as little as possible about the Christ mystery. Thus the Church had become an institution for keeping the Christ mystery secret, for as far as possible preventing the Christ mystery from reaching out into the world. This is something that must increasingly become clear to humanity at the present time, because this is the age when a start must be made with working with different concepts from those of Rome. Roman concepts are particularly inclined towards sharp outlines, sharp contours, the form of the corpse. Those concepts that are developed in order, for example, to understand man's true nature, in the way that I sketched the human aura on the blackboard for you here a week ago—ideas that are necessary in order to grasp man's true reality once more and thereby to some degree understand the true reality of the world—must be fluid in nature and not have sharp outlines, for the actual reality is not fixed but is in the process of becoming. If, therefore, we want to understand reality with our concepts and ideas, we must ensure that our concepts replicate the flow, the evolving nature of reality.

If this need for concepts to become mobile is ignored, what happens is that things can be observed in various places today which could prove disastrous for mankind. Take a phenomenon which an observer of the world who is wide awake and well grounded cannot fail to be aware of. It is as follows. We have among us in the world people of learning in all manner of different fields. These experts are the representatives and the guardians of knowledge, and people today, despite not being believers in authority and despite having rid the world of any such trust in authority, believe to the letter everything that is stated by these specialists in various areas of knowledge. And the experts among themselves always take on trust anything that is not in their particular field. People today do not like looking into such matters, because they would necessarily be struck by the ragged and chaotic nature of our culture. This is an example of the sort of thing that has been experienced. Let us suppose that a person of learning—and we could choose one from all the various areas of knowledge—has his own particular sphere, shall we say Egyptology (I want to take something a bit unusual). His profession is to instruct other people who are unable to study the sources of such knowledge concerning the distinctive qualities of the Egyptian people, and he also instructs them about the relationships of the Egyptians to the other peoples of antiquity. Those who receive this information are obliged to take it on trust, for the man is after all an authority on Egyptology. Now something most unfortunate is happening in our time: a large number of these learned individuals who represent specialist areas have not kept silent but have spoken about themes that do not belong to their particular subject. It would have been better if they had kept quiet, but they have not done so; they have, for instance, applied their thinking and their thought-forms under the impression of these events to their own nation and to its relations to other nations. One has now had sufficient opportunity to see what nonsense such individuals have been talking; and it is necessary to draw certain conclusions which are indeed grounded in reality. Many a person who is, shall we say, an authority in the realm of Egyptology and whose ideas about the distinctive qualities of the Egyptian people and their relationship to other peoples would be regarded as incontestable suddenly in our present time starts talking utter nonsense about his own nation and about the relation of his own nation to other nations. Do you really believe that such a person has been, and is now, talking any more sense about the Egyptians and about their relations with other peoples? When Balfour[2] speaks today about the relationship of his nation to the rest of the world, or when Houston Stewart Chamberlain[3] talks incessant rubbish about human relationships, one can gather without much reflection that they are talking complete and utter nonsense! But Chamberlain has now written *The Foundations of the Nineteenth Century* and a number of other books, the history of which there has not been the opportunity to verify. In these he has been talking exactly the same kind of nonsense.

The time has now come to examine everything, and specifically with a view to finally seeing that it is not simply a matter of making judgements that have a limited value, in that they are correct as far as they go (that is true of almost every judgement, even the most erroneous one is correct in a limited area), but that what really counts is to seek that flexibility of judgement that can be found only through spiritual science, which penetrates into the essence of reality.

It is remarkable what conflicts are manifested today between sound thinking and a thinking that is characteristic of our time. There has recently been news about a religious discussion that took place in Petersburg or Petrograd (as it has been called for a while, I don't know whether one should call it Petersburg again), thus a religious discussion that took place in the former St Petersburg. It is quite something to be hearing about a religious discussion happening in the midst of Bolshevism! Socialists, priests and of course all kinds of bourgeois folk were speaking about religion and its development. Of course, their remarks were not particularly intelligent. Nevertheless, much can be learnt from the discussion that they had there, which was of course tinged with a contemporary hue but was based thoroughly upon the most rigid and most ancient concepts. For example, a priest said something of the greatest interest. He feels himself—he said—obliged to address his flock as he was hitherto accustomed. What he used to say was that everything in the world—including Tsarism and all that goes with it—comes from God. What can this good priest do today? Of course he must somehow more or less adhere to what he used to say to his flock, even though they are no longer his flock, for he does not want to take on any new ideas. So he says: the world is from God, everything is from God. As we now have a Soviet government, that is also from God. Bolshevism has been sent by God to mankind. Since everything is from God, Bolshevism is also from God. What else was he to say? I am perfectly sure that the deductive reasoning could be taken further. Why should it not be made beautifully plausible that the devil is from God? According to these same inferences, the devil is appointed by God! It is indeed the case that one gains a deeper insight into what is needed, and that the strongest opposition can be met with in all areas of life. But one cannot go to sleep once one has undertaken to play a part in this remodelling of man's conceptual powers.

Concepts that have been developed out of materialism and are regarded as incontestable form part of what would need to be most thoroughly overcome. There is nothing that one encounters more often emanating from the so-called authority of science than what is known as the law of the conservation of energy and matter,[4] the conservation of force and of substance. This has entered deeply into mankind's heart. A world conception that has become wholly mechanistic and physical wants to be oblivious to the presence of the spirit; and as it has no wish to acknowledge the spirit it is also unable to ascribe either duration or eternity to the spirit, so it bestows eternity on its little idol, the atom, or to matter or to force in general. But the truth is that of all that you can perceive with your senses, of all that surrounds you both materially and as forces in the world, nothing will still be in existence after the Venus age according to the laws of the universe. We know that the Jupiter evolution follows that of the Earth, and the Venus evolution and then the Vulcan evolution will follow in its wake.[5] Just as man rediscovers himself in different incarnations, so the Earth will find itself anew as

Jupiter, after the Jupiter evolution as Venus and after the Venus evolution as Vulcan. What can be found today through experiments in
physics as matter and the structure of matter will no longer be there
after the Venus existence. There is no conservation of matter and of
energy—the matter and energy of which physicists speak—beyond
Venus existence. The whole law of the conservation of matter and of
energy is pure superstition, and this is what governs all concepts in
physics. But something is concealed when one speaks of the world as
consisting of indestructible substance that is constantly appearing in
different arrangements. This hidden 'something' is what emerges as the
answer to the question: What remains when everything that lies widely
outstretched before our senses will no longer be there, when the Venus
age has come or when it has reached its mid-point? What will then
remain? What can there possibly be that will be left?

Now direct your gaze towards all that you can survey outside you.
Look at everything, look at the totality of the mineral and plant
kingdoms, that of the animals and the world of man; look at all that you
can see of the starry heavens, all that is transmitted to you through
light, air and water; look wherever you will, bring together everything
that you can encompass in your outward sense-impressions and ask
yourself: where is there something that will remain of our present
existence? Not in any animal or plant or mineral or air or water,
nowhere but in man! Nothing of what you can see is included in what
will rightfully continue beyond Venus existence except man himself.
Nowhere else can you seek something permanent, something that can
be identified with the concept of eternity, other than in man. That is to
say, if we are searching for the seeds of the true future of the world,
where must we try to find them? We must search for them in man. We
can look for them in no other object of creation, in no kingdom of
nature. But through the kingdoms of nature people living in those
olden times before the Mystery of Golgotha perceived—spiritually, of
course—the cosmic universe. When they looked at the Sun, for
example, they beheld a fiery ball, but through the fiery ball they saw
Helios and the good. All the same, this fiery sphere of the Sun will not
continue in existence beyond the Venus age; it will then disappear. And
everything through which people in olden times saw the constituents of

some kind of spiritual existence as through a veil will likewise be gone. Of everything that now exists only what lives as a seedlike potential will remain for the future.

So what has actually happened? Before the Mystery of Golgotha human beings looked out into the far reaches of the universe; they saw stars upon stars, they saw the Sun and the Moon, air and water, the various kingdoms. But they did not see them in the same way as people do today; behind everything they perceived divine-spiritual existence and, moreover, the Christ, who had not yet descended to the Earth. In these ancient times people beheld Christ as part of the cosmos, as belonging to the extra-terrestrial world. Nothing of that world in which Christ was beheld will last beyond Venus existence. Everything through which the spiritual world and also the cosmic Christ were revealed to man in the times before the Mystery of Golgotha will last only until the Venus age. Before the Mystery of Golgotha human beings lived in close proximity with the heavens, but this heavenly world is so bound to the senses that it will also disappear with Venus existence. What will remain beyond Venus existence has its germinal essence only in man. Christ had to come to man from the cosmic expanses if He wished to embark with man on the path to eternity. It is because all this is as I have described it that Christ descended from the cosmos in order henceforth to unite with what will live on into eternity as a seed within man.

That is the great cosmic event that one has to understand. Before the Mystery of Golgotha people were able to venerate God and Christ in the cosmic expanses. Since then it has become increasingly the case that the seed for the future of the world resides only within man; and those people who were to come after the Mystery of Golgotha necessarily have a Christ who is not out there in a cosmos that is disintegrating but is united with man, with the human organism, with the human kingdom. It is literally true to say that what the senses perceive as stars, as heavenly bodies lying in the wide expanses of space, will pass away.[6] But the Word, the Logos, who has appeared in Christ and is united with man's eternal essential being, will remain. This is just as much a literal truth as those things that are imparted in genuine occult or religious documents are literal truths.

This is also the reason why there has to be a dualistic aspect in the name given to Christ Jesus, as I have already indicated. On the one hand one has to recognize the Christ who belongs to the extra-terrestrial cosmos, that spiritual Being who before the Mystery of Golgotha had no direct connection with human beings on the Earth; this should not be forgotten, for this Being has descended and has united Himself with human nature, with Jesus. In the dualistic name of Christ Jesus there lies what needs to be understood here. In the Christ one sees the cosmic, spiritual aspect; in Jesus one sees the means whereby this cosmic, spiritual Being entered into historical evolution and united Himself with mankind in such a way that He can now live on into eternity together with the germinal essence of man.

It was in a certain sense the task of the Church in the ensuing centuries to conceal and distort this mystery of Christ which was associated with the ancient mysteries. If you try to make a thorough study of the course of mankind's development in these centuries that have elapsed, if you try to see for yourself how human individuals have fared who really wanted to seek Christ Jesus, who really wanted to find the path to Him, it has always been a path of martyrdom. Christ Jesus has always had to be sought in defiance of convention, just as even today He must still be sought in the context of a battle against the conventions that still persist. But one cannot approach the mystery of Christ if one does not connect it with the mystery of nature.

The fact is that one can only understand what we have clearly identified as the need for Christ to descend from cosmic heights to man's germinal essence—the mystery of Christ becoming Jesus—if the study of nature, the study of the world, cosmology and a survey of human and divine evolution are brought together into a unity. There is a certain attitude of trying to prevent the study of the natural world from becoming at the same time a study of the divine and human world, and vice versa. This is what most theologians, and on the other hand most scientists, try to do today, namely to erect a barrier between natural science on the one side and the study of the divine and human world on the other. On no account is anything to be said about Christ Jesus that also has a bearing on earthly evolution, nor should anything be said about the evolution of the Earth, that is, about its various individual aspects, that is connected with the great spiritual mystery.

By touching on these things one is indeed venturing upon matters of the greatest, even supreme importance in human life today. For confused prattling about all sorts of spiritual matters, to which even our friends have frequently alluded and brought to our attention ad nauseam, is not of the slightest value. I am referring to the way that people constantly come and say: Look now, so-and-so has been speaking in a very theosophical or anthroposophical way, he has said such a thing! This facile quest for support in the present confusion is not what we ought to be aiming for; we should be standing firm on the foundation that spiritual science will give us. The times are too serious for further compromises, especially in this realm.

A bridge between the two realms of the knowledge of nature, that is, a knowledge of what we can perceive, and the knowledge of sin and redemption, in short, a knowledge which encompasses religious truths, can be built only if one finds the courage to break through into the spiritual world. But one cannot know anything of any value about the truths of life unless one has the courage to make inroads into the spiritual domain. A vital part of penetrating into the realities of the spirit is being able to look back to the threefold Sun mystery of ancient times, though in a new sense that is appropriate for people today. Just as the Sun has a trinity of aspects, man likewise has a threefold nature. But what matters is that we really study this threefold nature of man. This is what is most important for the present: studying threefold man. By way of preparation—tomorrow and the day after tomorrow we shall bring these studies to a conclusion—I should like to present to you something in schematic form that can guide you on the path that would have to be sought in order to understand man as a threefold being.

Just imagine the following (what I am sketching now is only meant as a diagrammatic presentation). Imagine that you had a form which is merely a picture, an image, something that has no significance in itself, just an image. I shall draw it like this: I am simply drawing a circle [see Diagram 1, blue], a circular area. This form is the image of something else, but through being an image it has completely consumed that something else of which it is an image. It may sound strange if I say what I am going to say, but just consider this. Four ladies are working in our cupola, in the small cupola; let us suppose that these four ladies, two

blau = blue   Head
                                                        gelb = yellow

Diagram 1

on either side, are painting portraits of one another, but that this activity has a particular consequence. So imagine these four ladies painting their portraits in the small cupola, painting pictures of one another; but that what they are engaged in has a quite definite sequel: they disappear by becoming one with their images; they cease to be there. Having completed their work they are no longer there. Through the coming into being of their images, they themselves cease to be there. Below what I have sketched here, picture to yourselves a form that has originated through being made by something of which it is the image; but through the existence of the image this something has been absorbed.

However, what has been thus absorbed is now not alone in the world. You need to imagine to yourselves that we have not yet finished with these four ladies. It is indeed so that these four ladies have disappeared, they have painted each other's portraits and disappeared; but the pictures are still there. They are not alone there in the universe, the universe is still there with all its forces. The ladies have vanished, they have as it were been sucked up by the pictures; but because the pictures are there, something of a substantial nature is drawn forth from the cosmos and forms the ladies anew, though now as children: they gradually come into being once more close by. Thus next to this form its archetype arises anew [see diagram, yellow]. I would have to make a little addition to the drawing, I shall draw it alongside: this is the archetypal image. This is the archetype or prototype, but there is a very loose connection between this image and its prototype, a very loose connection. They each have almost nothing to do with one another. This image has definitely hardened and has almost nothing to do with its prototype.

Now imagine a second form. I will sketch the second form in such a way that I draw it likewise as an image [see Diagram 2, violet], except that the first is inside the second. The first is something in its own right,

blau = blue 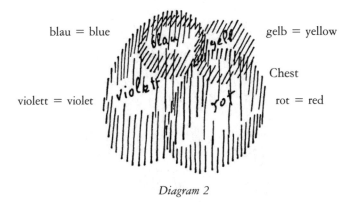 gelb = yellow

Chest

violett = violet   rot = red

Diagram 2

but it is also inside the second. Thus I am boldly drawing the second over the first. This is again an image of the same kind, similarly an image of another that I shall draw here also [see Diagram 2, red]; but I must connect it with this other one more closely. Since the situation now is such that I would not be able to choose the comparison that I chose earlier with the four ladies, if I was now to choose a suitable comparison for this picture and its image I would have to say: the four ladies are there, they are painting in the small cupola, and as they paint something actually goes out from them, is absorbed. They are, however, only half absorbed, and finally—well, I shall put it like this, so that the comparison has at least some aesthetic quality—from one of them the left half of the body is absorbed while the right is projected out of the picture; from the other the right side of the body is absorbed, while the left is still extending outwards. Thus they are partly absorbed and partly projected outwards. That is the second diagram.

Then imagine a third part of the composite drawing that again embraces the first and also the second [see Diagram 3, green]. This is, however, to a large extent connected with its image, it is not yet separated from it. So if I wanted to continue the comparison I would have to say: the ladies are painting, but they are also there as ladies, and everything that I have before me consists of the ladies and their images. That is depicted here [see Diagram 3, orange], and the large part of it is also present in the prototype.

So here [Diagram 1] you have, drawn somewhat diagrammatically, firstly in the top left position an image which has become hardened,

blau = blue

gelb = yellow

violett = violet

Limbs

rot = red

grün = green

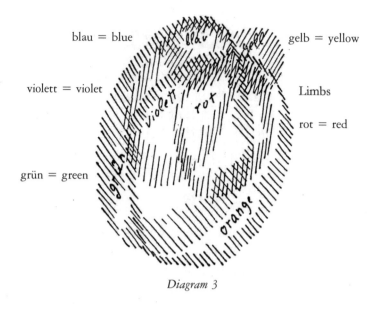

Diagram 3

crystallized and which has as little as possible to do with its prototype; this latter is next to it, newly arising. This is your head, the most material and the hardest part of human nature. Its prototype has absolutely nothing to do with it and is newly emerging; and when you reach 28 years of age your head is such that nothing further will be forthcoming from it, it is fully mature. The head is the greatest materialist in human nature. The second form is the chest and the breathing and everything belonging to it. This is approximately the way that I would delineate the second in diagrammatic form [see Diagram 2]. It is already more connected, spirit and matter are more interrelated and it is to a greater extent pervaded with spirit. The whole lung and breathing process is a more spiritual one for the Earth. And in the case of the remaining realm, that of the limbs, together with everything pertaining to sexuality, the spiritual domain is one with the physical, they are still together. This belongs to the third diagram.

This is threefold man. I have today only been able to draw it schematically on the blackboard. This mystery of threefold man, which is at once wonderful and rich with possibilities, majestic and far-reaching in its potential, is connected with the threefold mystery of the Sun. This again is connected with all the truths that we need—in the way that we need the bread of life—for everything that must be put in place of what has led to chaos, to a blind alley and to the present catastrophes afflicting mankind. We shall speak further of this tomorrow.

LECTURE 5

YESTERDAY I gave you a diagrammatic indication of threefold man. It is indeed the case that in the cultural life of modern times there is very little feeling for an understanding of man's being as it needs to be grasped from a spiritual-scientific standpoint. Nevertheless, we must make every effort to gain a clearer understanding of this being of man. For it is only out of such an understanding of the threefold nature of man's being that any ideas of real significance that we may acquire concerning not only the whole of human life but also man's development between death and a new birth can be sustained. Today we shall consider this threefold being of man in greater detail.

As we already indicated yesterday, the first object of our attention is the human head. In a certain sense this human head is really an independent form in its own right. You can position yourself in front of a human skeleton and see how easily the head can be detached, in that you can lift it off like a ball. In actual fact the division between the three members of human nature is not so simple that one could say that what can be so readily removed from the skeleton like a ball is the head part. These elements are not so strictly segregated as this. We need gradually to extricate ourselves from a purely diagrammatic understanding and also from what nature herself suggests to us to a living feeling. As you saw yesterday, I had to draw not three circles next to one another but one circle for the head, a second circle that overlapped the head and a third circle that overlapped both the other two. So if one were to represent threefold man diagrammatically in accordance with his physical nature, one would have to draw him thus: the head region [see the red circle A in the diagram], the trunk region [oval, yellow] and then the limb region [orange]—actually three spheres, even if these spheres are drawn out lengthwise. With the head region, hence with what is shown here as the red circle A, is connected the spiritual aspect, which is, as you saw yesterday, a youthful structure [small lightly hatched circle, white/yellow]. This spiritual aspect of the head is a youthful spiritual structure, whereas the head itself is an old physical structure, an essence with a physical form. Thus what is applied to man in general is totally appropriate for the head; even though it is not correct in this generalized form it is correct for the head. The white (spiritual) form that I have drawn here with respect to the head represents the time when you are asleep, out of the head. When you are awake it is united with the head and is for the most part inside the physical head. So it can very easily be separated from the physical head; it goes out of it and comes back in again.

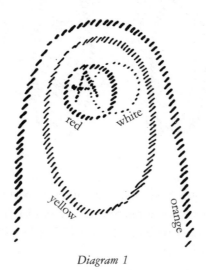

Diagram 1

This is certainly not the case for the middle—or chest—region of man's being. Everything enclosed by the thorax, by the ribs and backbone, is connected with the spiritual world, but this spiritual dimension is less markedly outside this region when you are asleep and remains closely connected with the physical body. As for the third region, that of the limbs, which also includes the sexual organs, there is barely any real separation between the sleeping and waking conditions. One certainly cannot say that the soul and spiritual aspects are disconnected in sleep, for they remain united to a greater or lesser degree. One could therefore draw a person in a waking state by means of another diagram and say that if this is his physical aspect in a waking condition [see Diagram 2a, dark hatching or red] this [lightly hatched or white form] would be its spiritual counterpart. And this would be someone who is asleep [see Diagram 2b, red and white]; the spiritual aspect is therefore united to a greater or lesser degree with the body, and only *this* particular part is really outside it [see Diagram 2b]. From a certain standpoint these would be appropriate drawings for showing the contrast between the states of waking and sleeping.

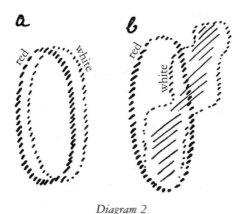

Diagram 2

Now you will only understand the important things that we have been speaking about if you relate this way of distinguishing the three aspects of man's being to another one which is linked with what I was explaining here last week.

If we reflect further over these three regions of the head, the trunk and the limbs, we can say that man's essential being is characterized solely by the trunk. It was therefore the living breath that was breathed into him by the Elohim. Breathing is his distinctive quality. The division here is not so simple as in the skeleton; the breathing process through nose and mouth forms part of this middle region of man's being. The differentiation is therefore not so easily represented diagrammatically as one would like to be able to draw it, but these are the sort of difficulties to be expected in understanding a matter of this kind.

Thus earthly man in his essential being is characterized by the trunk, while the head region, as a physical form, does not really have this distinctively human quality. One cannot say that the human head is quintessentially human. and indeed, it has something thoroughly ahrimanic about it. It is actually organized in the way it is because certain of its formative principles are a residue from Old Sun[1] and have therefore been left over from this second evolutionary stage of the Earth. Our head, in all its complexity of form, would not be as it is if it had not acquired its initial form in these ancient times of Old Sun. Hence these are old, primeval formative principles extending today into the earthly sphere, which for this reason must be described as ahrimanic. Residues of old principles always have to be regarded as luciferic or ahrimanic, according to their particular aspect. On the other hand, what makes man a citizen of the Earth, where the principles of earthly evolution are mainly at work, is that aspect of his being associated with the chest or trunk.

The limbs are also not wholly of a human nature but have a strongly luciferic quality, and their formative principles are not as yet complete in their development but will only have evolved to their full extent when the Earth has arrived at its Venus stage, thus when the preceding Jupiter stage has made the transition to the age of Venus. It will be then that the formative principles which today, I would say, still manifest only a shadow of the essential nature of this third aspect of man's being, that which relates to the extremities, will be active in their true form. Thus here man is anticipating what will only be a reality in the Venus age and manifests it in our time in an incomplete, germinal form which does not extend beyond something of a rudimentary nature.

This is how things appear from a cosmic standpoint. Thus from a cosmic point of view our human form is such that, as regards the forces involved, in our head we are repeating the period of Old Sun, whereas in our chest region we carry earthly evolution; and in so far as we live in the extremities we bear within us the seeds of Venus evolution. That is how it appears from a cosmic viewpoint.

From a human point of view it looks somewhat different. Here we must consider the human individuality as it progresses from one incarnation to another. In this context we must say that what we bear in this incarnation as our head has a relationship to our previous incarnation, what we now bear within us in the region of our chest is related purely to our present incarnation, and what we bear within our extremities already has a relationship to our next incarnation. I told you last week that the head has something very revealing about it, especially if viewed as a negative image.* If you were to take an impression of the physiognomy of the head and look at this physiognomy, you would recognize in this negative physiognomy of your head much of what you initiated in a former incarnation.

It is the opposite situation with the extremities. You cannot in this case take an impression but you have to adopt a different course. You need to think away the head and the trunk and instead consider everything that your hands and legs do; and of this you form for yourself a picture. You have to make a sort of map of this activity. You see, every time you do anything with your hands something happens elsewhere. You engage in activities and come in contact with other beings. If you were to paint all that your hands and legs do, if you were to draw a picture of what your hands and feet, arms and legs enact in the course of your life (and it would be a very lively picture!), you would discover a complicated map in this drawing; and from it you would find revealed what lies in store for you karmically in your next incarnation. From this map you would be able to discern much of the karma of your next incarnation. This is of profound significance. Just as the impression of the physiognomy in a state of rest, in the firm outlines of a drawing of it, reveals what happened in the previous incarnation, what one might be able to record of the way that arms, hands, legs and feet behave would be extraordinarily instructive with regard to what a person will do in his next incarnation—what he will carry out, where he will go, where his legs will take him. If you were to retrace all the steps that your legs have taken, a whole map would emerge from this. You would obtain some remarkable patterns. One's inclinations are not without influence on

---

* In the sense of the negative of a photographic image: Translator's note.

these patterns. Much of one's secret inclinations come to expression in them. These traces that remain are very revealing of what the next incarnation will bring to a person. So this is how to view it from a human perspective. Before this we were considering these phenomena from a cosmic viewpoint.

This way of understanding the different aspects of man's being, which is engendered from a present perspective, also implies a connection with the secrets of the ancient mysteries, where there was a more atavistic knowledge of these matters but where such secrets as have just been touched upon were already known. There is a beautiful legend relating to King Solomon about the certainty with which a person makes his way to the place where he is to meet his death. The meaning of this legend is that there is a particular place on the Earth where a person is to die, and he directs his footsteps to this place. (You will find a lecture where I spoke about this particular legend concerning Solomon.[2]) This is concerned with the ancient mystery knowledge of these things.

Now when someone is living in the ordinary way he only has his everyday consciousness; but man is, as you see, a highly complicated being. When he is awake, when his youngest spiritual member, the head, is within his physical head, he knows nothing of this head. You will rightly say: Thank God that we know nothing about the head; for if we know about the head this merely gives us a headache. People are only conscious of their heads when they have a headache; for then they know that they have a head. Otherwise they are unconscious of this— and to a remarkable degree, far more so than in the case of any other part of the human physical body. A person may be very glad if in normal consciousness he knows nothing of his head. But beneath this consciousness of the head, which normally has cognizance only of the outer world, which sets out to know only what is in its vicinity, lies another kind of consciousness, a dream consciousness or knowledge. Your head is continually dreaming. While you are aware of the outer world in the way that you are well familiar with, you are actually perpetually dreaming beneath the threshold of consciousness, in the region of the subconscious. And what you are dreaming in this head of yours, if you were able fully to grasp it and bring it into your conscious awareness, would give you a picture—and an accurate, comprehensive picture—of your previous incarnation; for in your head you are subconsciously dreaming of your previous incarnation. This is indeed so. There is always a slight awareness of this, a dreamy awareness of one's former incarnation, which is overpowered by the stronger light of everyday consciousness.

By the year 747 before the Mystery of Golgotha this outer consciousness had become so strong that this subconscious awareness of one's previous incarnation had gradually been completely extinguished. Before that year, however, much was known about this dream consciousness of the head. This is why you find that at the foundations of ancient cultures repeated earthly lives were everywhere adduced as a fact. This is simply because this subconsciousness of the head had not at that time receded so completely into the background, as happened throughout the fourth, but is now proceeding apace during the fifth post-Atlantean epoch.

It is also the case that very little is known in ordinary consciousness about the soul and spiritual associations of the thorax and the trunk, or man's middle region. It has in itself something of a dream quality. Only on occasion, and then very chaotically and irregularly, does this thorax consciousness thrust its way into a person's dream consciousness. If someone is able to breathe regularly, if his heartbeat is even and if all the functions of his middle region are in order, the consciousness of this aspect of his being is not as clear as that of the head; for even in ordinary life it has a dreamlike quality. As I have explained here in the past year,[3] we dream in our feelings of this middle region of our human nature. But when what lives in the feelings—and can be experienced only in this realm—is elevated through a consciousness that becomes increasingly clairvoyant, when, in other words, a person learns consciously to survey what is going on in his thorax in the way that he is otherwise only able to survey what lives in his head consciousness while he is awake, this thorax consciousness, that consciousness that lives in the trunk of the middle region of man's being, splits into two distinct parts. One part dreams back into the whole time between the previous death and the present birth or conception. Thus whereas in very deep dreams in your head consciousness you have a subconscious experience of your previous incarnation, in the dreams of the thorax you have an experience of what has in the meantime elapsed since that previous incarnation and your present birth. And in the dreams that belong more to the lower part of the thorax you have a powerful awareness of what lies between your impending death and the next earthly life. Thus the consciousness that is concentrated in the thorax, of which people today are largely unaware, is in reality a dream consciousness both of the time before this birth and of the time after this death. Thus the solution to the riddle of what lies between our last earthly death and our next earthly incarnation, with the exception of or even including what we are now experiencing between birth and death, may be found in the subconscious life of the middle region of man's being.

And in a realm of experience which remains in a deep state of unconsciousness throughout one's life and which can be brought to light only if a person is able to call it forth through constant work with spiritual-scientific studies and exercises, so that certain moments of sleep life which would otherwise pass unconsciously in a state of sleep are drawn to the surface and the person concerned becomes conscious during sleep, the tableau of the next earthly incarnation can be summoned forth from the third region of human nature, from the subconscious realm of the limbs or extremities. The ordinary waking consciousness that people have today is really a kind of subordinate impulse which streams into the head from without. However, behind this consciousness there lies another which extends over the previous incarnation, over the life from that incarnation to the next, present one and then again over the next incarnation. But people sleep through any awareness of this.

In the head there lives the consciousness of the previous incarnation. In all the organs that pre-eminently serve the function of out-breathing there works a strong consciousness of the life between the previous incarnation and this one. In all the functions that contribute to in-breathing there is a consciousness that extends from the present incarnation to the next earthly incarnation. And in the limbs, in all the mysterious processes of this system of the body, there exists a deeply unconscious awareness of the next incarnation.

These states of consciousness have become more or less veiled since the beginning of the fourth post-Atlantean epoch, since 747 before the

Mystery of Golgotha. The challenge of our time is to summon forth the specific awareness of these various processes of cosmic and human evolution from the general chaos of human consciousness today.

What I have just been explaining needs to be complemented by another insight into the being of man. It is indeed necessary that we involve ourselves in the discussion of these difficult matters, otherwise we will be unable to arrive at a clear understanding. I would be pleased if these difficult themes were not merely greeted with a certain passive acceptance but if, specifically for these matters which are hard to understand (and are yet so important for people today), a little enthusiasm, a little lively interest were aroused, which is a very tall order indeed in any society today.

Now consider, you direct your senses towards the outer world; by means of your senses you find the outer world spread out as a perceptible phenomenon. I will make a diagrammatic representation of what lies outspread around us as a sense-perceptible impression. Let this [see Diagram 3, blue] be what is out there around us. When you direct your eyes, your ears, your sense of smell or whatever sense you choose towards the outer world, the inner aspect of this outer world turns towards you, towards your senses. This, then, is the inner aspect of the outer world [left]. Suppose you turn your senses towards what I have drawn [see diagram, arrows]; these senses are directed towards the outer world and you see here what is inwardly oriented. Now follows the difficult notion that I need to explain. Everything that you behold there is manifesting itself to you from within. You may suppose that it must also have an outward aspect. I should like to give you some sort of a picture of this by saying that when you look outwards in this way you see the firmament—the vault of heaven—as the limit of your perception: it is something like this, except that I have drawn it on a miniature scale. But now imagine that you could fly out there, fly through all this and look from the other side, look at your sense impressions from the other side. Thus you could look in this sort of way [see diagram, upper arrows]. Of course, you do not see this; but if you could look in this way, it would be this other aspect. You would have to go outside yourself and look at the whole of your sense-perceptible world from the other side. So you would see what presents itself to you as colour from the far side,

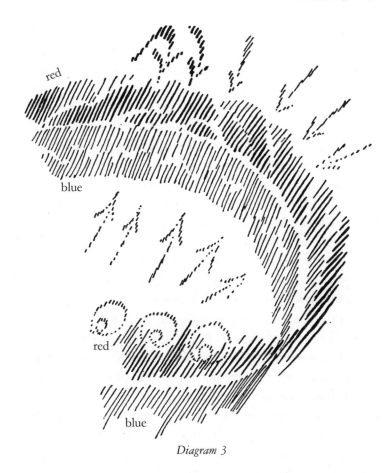

Diagram 3

what presents itself to you as sound from the far side and so on. Similarly, you would behold what comes towards you as smell from yonder side, you would sniff it with your nose from this yonder side. Just imagine contemplating the world from the other side: imagine sense-perceptible objects spread out like a carpet, and that the carpet is now seen from the other side. You see only a little bit, a very, very little bit of this yonder side. It is possible for me to depict this little bit only in this way. Imagine now that what I am drawing in red is what you would see from the other side, so that I can say that the world of sense-perceptions can be portrayed diagrammatically as follows: to one's ordinary perception it appears blue; viewed from the other side it appears red, though of course one does not see this. In what you would see as red is, in the first instance, hidden everything that can be experienced between death and a new birth and, secondly, all that is described in *An Outline of Occult Science*[4] as the evolutions of Saturn, Sun, Moon, Earth and so forth. It is a kind of storehouse of what is concealed from sense-perceptible vision. There it is on the other side of the sphere; but you see only a little bit of it. I can best indicate this by saying: take this little section of the red and let it cross over [see diagram, above] and intersect with the blue, so that the blue instead of being, as now, in front is behind. I would have to draw this four-dimensionally if I were to draw it *in accordance with reality*; so I can only depict it in a very schematic way. Thus *here* [left] the senses are directed towards the blue; whereas *there* they are directed towards not the blue but the red, which you do not otherwise see. But what is normally seen has crossed over behind the red, and is now beneath it; and you see this little bit that crosses the other continually with your ordinary consciousness. These are your stored up memories. Everything that arises as memory arises not in accordance with the laws of this world of outer perception but in accordance with the laws corresponding to this world that lies behind that other world. This inner realm that equates with your memories actually corresponds to what is on the other side [right]. When you look into yourself and delve into your memories, you are indeed seeing one portion of the world from the other side; this other side projects inwards a little and then you see the world from the other side. And if you were now able to slip through your memories as they have been inscribed in this way (I spoke about this a week ago), if you were able to go down there and look beneath your memories and see them from the other side,[5] from over there [see Diagram 2, Lecture 2, left], you would see the memories as your aura. You would then see man as a being with a soul-spiritual aura, as you otherwise behold the outer world of sense-perceptions. But as I indicated here last week, this would not be particularly pleasant; because when viewed from this other side man is not yet beautiful to look at.

So this is an interesting adjunct to our other knowledge of threefold man. The intersection here lies in the middle region of man's being, that of the chest. You remember the drawing that I made a week ago,[6] where I had the coiled up lemniscates with their inverted loops: I would have to draw these here. I would need to draw this middle region of man's being with these inverted lemniscates [see Diagram 3, above left]; this would coincide with the sphere of memory. So in his middle region this threefold being of man has this capacity to turn inside out, where inner becomes outer and the outer becomes inner; where what you would otherwise behold as a cosmic tableau, as the great cosmic memory, you now see as your own little microcosmic memory. You see in your ordinary consciousness what has occurred from your third year onwards until now: this is an inner record, a small part of what is of a similar nature to it and which constitutes a record of the whole of world evolution, and which lies on the other side.

It was not without reason that—as most of you will be well aware—I once spoke with you about the fact that man actually has twelve senses; and I also mentioned this in the notes at the end of my last book *The Riddles of the Soul*.[7] We should think of these senses in such a way that several of them are directed towards the sense-perceptible, while others have an opposite orientation. These are directed towards what is already inverted [see Diagram 3, at the bottom]. Those directed towards what is outwardly sense-perceptible are: the senses of ego, thought, language (speech or the word), hearing, sight, taste and smell. The other senses, on the other hand, do not engage with man by way of his consciousness, because their orientation is towards his inner being and towards the opposite aspect of the world. These are the senses of warmth, life, balance, movement and touch. Hence we can say that for the ordinary consciousness seven senses lie in the light [upper part of Diagram 4] and five senses in the dark [lower part]. And the five senses lying in the dark are turned towards the other side of the world, and also towards the other side within man [see Diagram 3].

Hence there is a complete parallel between the senses and between something else of which we shall speak in a moment [see Diagram 4, circle]. So if we accept that we need to list as senses those of hearing, language, thought, ego, warmth, life, balance, movement, touch, smell, taste and sight, we have essentially those senses ranging [in the diagram] from the sense of ego to the sense of smell which lie in the light, in what is accessible to ordinary consciousness [see the hatched area of Diagram 4]. And everything that is turned away from ordinary consciousness, as night is turned away from day, belongs to the other senses.

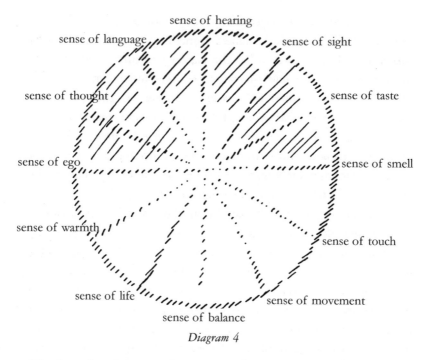

Diagram 4

The boundary between the two is only approximate, there is some overlapping; reality is not always so accommodating. But this way of ordering man's being according to the senses is such that you need merely to draw in place of the names of the senses the signs of the zodiac, Ram, Bull, Twins, Crab, Lion, Virgin, Scales—seven signs for the light side, and five for the dark side—Scorpion, Archer, Goat, Waterman, Fishes: day, night; night, day. And you have a complete parallel between microcosmic man—with on the one hand what is oriented towards his senses and, on the other, what is turned away from them but is oriented towards his lower senses—and what in the outer cosmos signifies the alternation from day to night. What takes place within man is the same as what is enacted in the whole structure of the cosmos. In the cosmos day alternates with night, and within man there is also an alternation between day and night, namely waking and sleeping, even though both may have separated themselves from one another for the present cycle of human consciousness. During the day man is oriented towards the day senses; we can just as well equate this with the Ram, Bull, Twins, Crab, Lion, Virgin and Scales as with the senses of ego, thought, language and so on. You can see the ego of every other person, you can understand the thoughts of another person, you can hear, see, taste, smell—these are the day senses. In the night man is oriented towards the other senses, in the same way that the Earth is turned towards the other side, only these are not yet fully developed. Only after the Venus age will they be so fully developed that they are able to perceive what is on the other side. They are shrouded in night, just as the Earth is in the shadow of night as it passes through the other regions of the heavens, through the other signs of the zodiac. Man's journey through his senses is a parallel course to that of the Sun around the Earth (or of the Earth around the Sun, it makes no difference which we choose in this case); these phenomena are indeed connected. And those who bore the wisdom of the ancient mysteries were well familiar with these connections.

This gradually vanished from consciousness in the fourth post-Atlantean epoch, but it must be revived once again; despite the resistance that rises up amidst modern culture, it needs to be reinstated there. For in the concepts that one acquires there it becomes very possible to understand what is happening now in the outward tapestry of social life. So long as you separate the life of nature and the life of the spirit, or the inner world, in the way that present-day humanity loves to do, you do not arrive at concepts that could play a part in historical evolution but you are instead overwhelmed by the concepts that predominate in the outward affairs of humanity today. Overwhelmed! There are many examples of this.

It is indeed the case that in the course of, say, the last couple of centuries people have done an incredible amount of thinking. It would be possible to gather up what people have been thinking for the last two hundred years, what ideals they have formulated, ideals which they have regarded—and continue to regard—as being great, ranging from the ideal of the Age of the Enlightenment to that of the great would-be Caesar, Woodrow Wilson. Everything that has been said about the various ideals has come out of the thoughts that people have been having over the centuries, specifically these last two centuries; this has been forming people's thoughts. World history is, however, affected only to a small degree by these thoughts. It is stirred by something altogether different: by those thoughts that have been working and weaving in actual realities. And never have the thoughts that buzz around in people's heads been further removed from the great cosmic thoughts that live in actual realities than in our time. What has been inspiring human beings for, say, the last 150 years in order to fashion the world in a certain way have not been the ideals of freedom, equality, brotherliness, justice and so forth but thoughts that are interwoven with, for example, the advent of the power loom. That the power loom became part of modern developments in the second half of the eighteenth century, that this significant invention of the power loom entered into human evolution in place of the traditional method of weaving by hand and the whole mechanistic culture of modern times arose from this power loom are symptoms of the objective thoughts, the real thoughts, that have given the world the form that it still has today and out of which the catastrophic chaos of the present has emerged. If one is seeking to write a history of the catastrophic chaos of the present, one should not turn to the thoughts that have been buzzing around in people's heads but to these objective thoughts of the founding, the inventing of the power loom and on to the growth of big industry and its shadow, socialism; for although big industry and socialism appear to be opposites, they are polar opposites that belong together and should not be separated. These objective thoughts need to form the basis of our consultations and our observations of historical development.

One then finds that in the course of the eighteenth and nineteenth centuries and especially in that part of the twentieth century in which we are now living people entertained a number of illusions. However, although they had these illusions in their thoughts, they were overwhelmed by the objective, cosmic thoughts underlying history. These thoughts are weaving in actual realities. The only people who have really been developing a gradual interest in these objectively weaving thoughts, albeit a terribly one-sided one, are those who have formed socialism as a world view. That is something hugely characteristic. If you follow the course of the nineteenth century, the bourgeoisie has increasingly been losing interest in great questions of world views. Such questions are indeed becoming highly distasteful to the bourgeoisie; where possible they shift them to the realm of aesthetics. The average member of the bourgeoisie, or middle class, is happy to hear all sorts of views in the theatre as to whether spiritual beings exist or not, when there is no need to believe in them and when it does not matter whether something is true or not; and so Bjørnson[8] and people like him are allowed to get away with saying all manner of things. Thus in recent times matters relating to world views have as far as the bourgeoisie is concerned been dispatched to the realm of aesthetics, to the frivolity of what purports to be art. Where people have in the last few years really been breaking their—and others'—heads open with respect to questions of world views is in the name of socialism. (I am not advocating this as an ideal in the physical sense, but in an inner, spiritual sense—it is in a certain sense a worthy aim; as you know, I have given very emphatic hints to the effect that I would welcome a lively mood even where anthroposophical truths are being discussed.) Other people, on the other hand, have taken no notice of this. They have, I would say, disregarded those people who have actually been looking at the world from a very narrow point of view, who have been seeing the world only from the standpoint of the factory, from the inside of factories, from the inside of a printing works and so forth. Of course it is highly interesting to observe what kind of a so-called world view has emerged from the standpoint of the factory: for that is what socialism is! It derives from the inside of the factory, from people who have no knowledge of anything except the inside of a factory. And the bourgeoisie, with all its abstract ideas, though abstract ideas tinged with aestheticism so that one does not need to try so hard breaking one's head open, has little interest in what is being developed in this context. Curiously, therefore, the bourgeoisie finds itself in the middle between the totally moribund old world view which has lost every trace of the spiritual aspect and would like to assign all questions of significance to the realm of aesthetics and what has newly emerged in the form of socialism, which has no concepts whatsoever and founds systems on mere words, on the grounds that it is unable to see the world but can see only the factory and, moreover, the most external aspect of its mechanical side. Just imagine what it actually means if man inwardly knows nothing about the mineral, plant and animal kingdoms and knows only about the way in which a certain cock in a machine is moved mechanically up and

down, this or that is filed and planed and so on! Socialism is a world
view based on the perception of a world which is purely mechanical. For
the socialist, that part of the world which is mechanical has been cut
out; and he forms his concepts in accordance with this part which has
been thus extracted.

This has been allowed to arise through the principle having been
adopted that one should concern oneself with things only through the
medium of aesthetics. When the Theosophical Society was first established its basic principle was seen as being the love of all people for one
another. What a lot has been proclaimed about this! I have myself had
plenty to say on this theme. It is as easy to do this as it is fruitless. But
this is also because people like wherever possible to shift something that
has real content into a realm where there is no actual substance. So there
could also be no genuine interest in the true course of events. Certain
individuals, however, have been struck by the peculiar nature of what
we may refer to as the conventional way of studying history. Let us take
an example.

Take any account of the time of the Roman Caesars, and try to learn
about this period from textbooks or in the books that the great
authoritative historians have written. I believe that you will hear very
little indeed from these sources about a certain personality who played
an important political part under Nero[9] (for even under Nero it was
possible to have political aspirations) and then aroused quite special
attention and wielded considerable influence on Roman politics under
Vespasian[10] and Titus,[11] so that one can say that this personality was
the soul of the governments of Vespasian and Titus. Then this personality reverted to the other side under the reign of Domitian,[12] whom
he regarded as damaging to Rome. Accordingly a lawsuit was brought
against him, a lawsuit that made a great stir in Rome and unfolded in a
very interesting way; for Domitian suddenly changed from a tyrant to
someone who was at his wits' end in the case and was therefore unable to
pass judgement on the man. And then when Nerva[13] succeeded
Domitian, we see this personality again actively associated with the
Emperor, the Caesar. So we see this personality exerting considerable
political influence out of the world view of that time, and at the same
time we see him making a last attempt within the context of the Roman

Empire to implant truly far-reaching concepts brought down from the cosmos into political events. What is curious is that one does not find a proper description of this personality in any ordinary history book, not even in Suetonius[14] or Tacitus[15], but only in Philostratus;[16] and even Philostratus describes him in such a way that one does not know whether he is writing a novel or describing a historical figure. He gives an account of the life of Apollonius of Tyana.[17] For it is Apollonius of Tyana of whom I have been speaking to you as having had so great an influence on politics from Nero to Nerva and especially under Vespasian and Titus; and he is described by Philostratus. Baur,[18] the theologian and historian from Tübingen, was utterly astonished that one finds absolutely nothing about a figure such as Apollonius, who should rightly play a leading part in any historical account. Of course, Baur did not have any insight into why this is so; for the point here is that we have in Apollonius a historical figure who indeed had this great influence but who brought the principles out of which he worked down from the cosmic expanses. This was highly embarrassing for the Christianity that was emerging at the time of the Roman Empire. And now I beg you to consider that everything that is inscribed in history is there by the grace of the Church. Nothing is there except what man has been allowed to have by the grace of the Church. Not without reason did an old and by no means stupid man assert that there never was a Plato or a Sophocles but that monks in the fourteenth and fifteenth centuries had written the plays of Sophocles; for there is no absolute proof that Sophocles ever lived. Even though the assertion is untenable and is, of course, nonsense, we have nevertheless often emphasized how uncertain the accepted version of history is. And we should be quite clear about it. We must indeed bring the present into connection with the past, for we are now approaching a great and highly significant question.

We have, now from a modern standpoint, once again referred to the threefold being of man, to his connection with cosmic truths and to the need for these truths to be once more unveiled. And what has the principal activity of the Church been, especially since the eighth Ecumenical Council in Constantinople that took place in 869? It has been to obliterate and eradicate from human consciousness any understanding that likewise Christianity had in those ancient times of man's connection with the cosmos and with the wider spiritual world. Everything betraying any hint of this connection has been eliminated with a real sense of alarm. And only because not everything can be eradicated, on the grounds that karma counteracts such a tendency, have such works as those of Philostratus survived. You can therefore understand that if you now bring the past into connection with the present, certain people belonging to the Church will become terribly worried if efforts are made in the present to form a link between what makes man a cosmic being and this earthly human being himself together with his task.

It is not acceptable that what should be the will of the anthroposophical movement is pursued in no more than a dulled state of consciousness; for it is necessary that it is taken up in a fully vital and vigorous way. I have now given an indication of what we will explore further. Tomorrow I shall give here the lecture in which I shall take the thread of these observations forward.

LECTURE 6

DORNACH, 26 AUGUST 1918

CERTAIN questions increasingly thrust themselves on the attention of thinking people, even though in these times when a materialistic culture predominates they would on the whole prefer to ignore them. There are many such questions. Today I should like to select a few from the considerable number of questions that arise by virtue of the fact that, despite the resistance that people have to becoming aware of a spiritual world, they nevertheless sense its presence. Among such questions are these, for example, which are brought up in the course of everyday life. Some people die young, others die when they are really old, others somewhere in between. With regard to this fact that on the one hand young children die and on the other hand people become quite old before they die, questions arise in people's minds which, as everyone would need to admit if they really thought about it, cannot be answered with what are today called scientific means. Nevertheless these are urgent questions for human life, and surely anyone can sense that an immense number of things in life would be clarified if one could address questions such as why some human beings die early, whether as children, as adolescents or in the prime of life, and why others die when they are old. What significance does this have for the world as a whole?

People still had ideas and concepts for answering such questions until that point of time to which I have already drawn your attention in these lectures, that is, the beginning of the fourth post-Atlantean epoch (roughly the middle of the eighth century BC). These concepts were a legacy of ancient wisdom. In those ancient times that preceded the eighth pre-Christian century, ideas that gave people answers to questions such as those indicated in a way that they could understand were circulating throughout the earthly cultures of that time. What we call science today has no way of approaching such questions and does not even consider that there is any reason why one should look for an answer to them. This is due to the fact that in the period that has elapsed since the point of time indicated, all ideas relating to the spiritual or immortal aspect of man's being have actually been lost. The only ideas that remain are those that have a bearing on man's transient nature, that part of human nature that is encompassed between birth and death.

I have pointed out that in all ancient conceptions of the world people spoke of a threefold Sun—referring as they did to that same Sun that one perceives as a radiant sphere out in space. However, behind this Sun the sages of olden times saw the soul aspect of the Sun (which the Greeks called Helios) and behind this again the spiritual Sun, which Plato, for example, identified with the good.[1] People today do not see any real sense in speaking of Helios, the soul aspect of the Sun, or for that matter of the spiritual Sun, of the good. But just as the physical Sun shines upon us here between birth and death, so, I must emphasize, does the spiritual Sun, which Plato identifies with the good shed its light upon our ego in the time that we spend between death and a new birth. It makes no sense to speak of this radiant sphere associated with our modern materialistic world view in relation to the time between death and a new birth; during this time it only makes sense to speak of the spiritual Sun referred to by Plato as the good. But it is precisely this kind of concept which is able to point us in the right direction. It can enable us to subject our physical conception of the world to critical examination. No serious consideration would, after all, be given to the notion— or at any rate not to the point where our outlook on life were to be influenced by it—that the physical representations that we form of the world, what is spread out before our senses, are a kind of illusion, a sort of maya.

Thus anyone who regards modern physics (or astrophysics if you prefer) as authoritative conceives of the Sun in the following way. If he were able to go to where physicists place the Sun, he would on approaching the Sun (we may for present purposes ignore the circumstances of human life and consider the conditions from an absolute point of view) become aware of an immense heat, this is how he would imagine it; and on arriving within the space that physicists conceive as being filled by the Sun he would find in this space something of the nature of fiery gas. This is how a physicist would think of it—a fiery ball of gas or something of the kind. But it is not like that; such an idea is maya, a complete illusion. It does not even stand up to the scrutiny of such physical perception as can be achieved, never mind any real supersensible perception. If one were really able to get close to the Sun and enter the space where the Sun is, one would, on approaching it, find something that has a similar effect to going through floods of light [a drawing was made of a yellow circle with a blue centre]; but if one were fully to enter the place where physicists imagine the physical Sun to be, one would initially find what one might identify as empty space. There is nothing there at all; there is absolutely nothing where the physical Sun is supposed to be. I shall draw it diagrammatically [blue], because nothing is actually there at all. Nothing is there, only empty space. But what a strange empty space it is! When I say that nothing is there, I am not speaking altogether accurately; for there is less than nothing there. It is not merely an empty space but it contains less than nothing. An idea of this nature is extraordinarily difficult for modern westerners to picture. Someone from the East would even today accept such an idea as a matter of course; for him there is nothing miraculous or difficult to understand if one were to say to him that less than nothing is there. The westerner thinks to himself—especially if he is a devoted follower of Kant, and far more people are Kantians, unconscious Kantians, than one might suppose—that if nothing is in a space, it must therefore be an empty space! But this is not the case; a space can also be emptied out. If you were to look through the Sun's corona, you would find the empty space that you would then enter most uncomfortable; for it would tear you apart. In this way it manifests its actual nature, that it is more—or, as I would rather say, less—than an empty space. You need only to avail yourselves of the simplest mathematical concepts in order to cease finding what I am trying to say so puzzling: that an empty space is less than merely being empty. Let us suppose that you possess a property of some kind. It may also happen that you have given away what you possess and have nothing. But one can also have less than nothing; one can have debts, and then one truly has less than nothing. One can go from a space that is totally full to one that is ever less so, until one ends up with an empty space; and one can then go beyond mere emptiness in the same way that one can go from nothing to having debts.

That is the great misconception of the modern world view, that it does not recognize this distinctive kind of negative materiality (if I may use such an expression), that it recognizes only emptiness and fullness and not what is less than emptiness. It is because knowledge in our time, the modern world view, has no understanding of what is less than emptiness that this same modern world view is to all intents and purposes shackled to materialism, well and truly shackled to materialism or—I might even say—under its spell. For there is also a place within man, I may say, which is emptier than empty; not in its totality but which has parts that are emptier than empty. Man—I am referring now to the physical human being—is as a whole a being who materially fills a space; but a certain member of human nature, of the three to which I have referred, does indeed have something about it which is like the Sun, emptier than empty. This is—and I am afraid you'll just have to accept it—the head. It is just because man is organized in such a way that his head can become empty and in certain parts of it can be emptier than empty that the head has the possibility of making room for the spiritual dimension of life. Just picture the reality of this situation. Of course, this has to be done diagrammatically; but you may imagine that everything materially filling your head is indicated diagrammatically by what I am about to draw. This would be your head [see diagram, red]. But if I am going to draw it properly, I shall have to leave some empty spaces in this head. These are of course not so big, but there are empty spaces inside it; and into these empty spaces what I have over the course of these days referred to as the youthful spirit can enter. This youthful spirit, in the form of its rays, is then incorporated in the drawing [yellow].

Now the materialists say that the brain is the instrument of the soul-life, of the thinking. The opposite is true: the holes in the brain, what are more than holes (or, I could also say, less than holes), are the instrument of the soul-life. And where there is no soul-life, where the soul-life is

red

yellow

Diagram 1

continually impinging, where the space in our skull is filled with the substance of the brain, nothing is thought, nothing is experienced by the soul. We need our physical brain not for our life of soul, we need it merely in order that we can take hold of our soul-life, physically take hold of it. If the soul-life that actually lives in the holes of the brain were not everywhere pushing against what is around it, it would vanish, it would never reach our consciousness. But it lives in the holes of the brain, which are emptier than empty.

So we must gradually correct our concepts. When we are standing in front of a mirror, we do not perceive ourselves but only our reflected image. We can forget ourselves: we see ourselves in the mirror. In the same way a person does not experience himself by assembling with his brain what lies in the holes of the brain; he experiences the way in which his soul-life is reflected whenever it comes up against the substance of the brain. This reflective process takes place everywhere, and this is what a person experiences; he is actually experiencing the reflected image of his soul-life. Whereas what slips through into the holes is that which then, once a person has passed through the gate of death, becomes conscious of itself without the resistance of the brain, because in that situation it is imbued with consciousness in a completely opposite sense.

I shall now draw another diagram, which I can portray as follows. Forgive me if I now draw the brain, somewhat drastically, so that I allow for the holes [blue]. Here is the substance of the brain, allowing space for the holes, and into these holes goes the life of the soul [yellow].

The soul-life, however, continues apart from the holes. In this way we come to the human aura, which is naturally only visible in close proximity to a person but extends to an indeterminate degree.

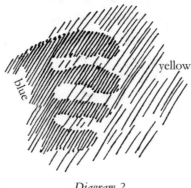

Diagram 2

Let us now think away the brain, and imagine that we are observing the soul-life of an ordinary person between birth and death. We would have to say that, seen in this way, the person as he actually is between birth and death is such that—and it is clear that I shall have to draw this in a different way diagrammatically—his face is turned like this towards his body [Diagram 3, lilac]; his soul-life is inclined towards his bodily existence. And when we look at the brain this soul-life stretches out feelers which enter the holes of the brain. What I formerly [see Diagram 2] depicted in yellow I am now drawing in lilac, because this is more appropriate for a perception of a living person. It would be this that extends into the brain of a living human being.

If I were now to draw a physical person, I would best be able to indicate this by showing the boundary to which the faculty of memory extends. It would reach outwards at this point, and this would be the outer boundary, the boundary of cognition, of which I have also spoken to you. You will need here to recall the previous diagrams and the third diagram that I drew yesterday.

But now it is indeed the case that if one contemplates man spiritually from without his soul-life extends into him *thus*. I shall therefore draw the single extending line only with respect to the brain. But this soul-life is also differentiated. So if I were to continue my investigation of the life of the soul, I would need to draw another region here [red under the lilac] and another one here [blue]; thus all this would form part of what constitutes the human aura. Then another region [green]: you see that this part that I am now drawing lies beyond the limits of human cognition. Then this region [yellow] and this region [orange] all actually belong to the human individual.

When a person is asleep this moves more or less out of the body, as was drawn yesterday [Diagram 2] and when he is awake it is more or less within the body, so that the aura can be perceived in a soul sense only in the immediate vicinity of the body. In describing man's physical organism one would say that the physical human being consists of lungs, heart, liver, gall bladder and so on. This is what the anatomist or the physiologist would say. One can in a very similar way describe the soul and spiritual aspect of man's being, which extends in this way into the holes within man, into what is more than empty within him. You can describe this equally well. But you must then state what this soul-spiritual aspect of man's being consists of. For just as organs can be distinguished in man's physical organism, so here can one distinguish particular streams. One can say that where I have drawn the red the physical human being would be standing thus in profile, the face would be turned in this direction, the eyes would be here [see Diagram 3]; and here would be the region of burning desires [red]. This would be one element of man's soul-spiritual being which has derived its substance from the region which you know from *Theosophy*[2] as that of burning desires. Thus a certain aspect of burning desires that has been incorporated into man gives rise to this part of him.

If I am going into detail, I would have to characterize what I have drawn here in lilac as the soul-life. As you know, a certain part of the soul realm, the soul-land, is referred to as the 'soul-life'. Its substance would be this violet or lilac area, which forms part of man's soul-spiritual being. What I have drawn in orange would—if we continue naming them all—be called the active soul force. So you would have to imagine that what enters into you by way of your senses in the course of the life between birth and death is your soul-life; and behind is the active soul force, holding itself back, not thrusting forward and held up by the soul-life. Still further behind is what we can call the soul light and forcing its way through would be that which is derived from the region of attraction and repulsion. I would have to associate this with the green area [see diagram]. Then the realm of wishes would have a bluish tinge; and then thrusting itself up against the blue but tending more towards a bluish red would be the region of flowing susceptibility. What I refer to

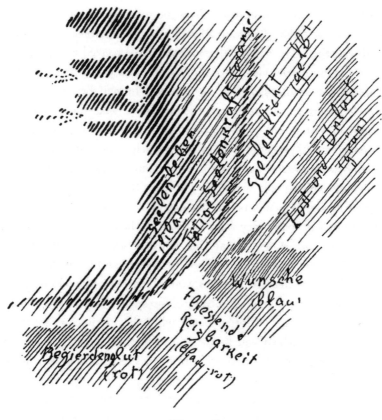

Diagram 3

Seelenleben (lila)	=	soul-life (lilac)
Tätige Seelenkraft (orange)	=	active soul force (orange)
Seelenlicht (gelb)	=	soul light (yellow)
Lust und Unlust (grün)	=	attraction and repulsion (green)
Wünsche (blau)	=	wishes (blue)
Fliessende Reizbarkeit (blau-rot)	=	flowing susceptibility (bluish red)
Begierdenglut (rot)	=	burning desires (red)

here as burning desire, flowing susceptibility and wishes are auric streams. As you know, these auric streams constitute the soul-world; but they also make up man's soul-spiritual being, which is composed of the elements of this soul-world.

At death the physical body falls away and the individual human being withdraws what has extended itself into the physical body by way of the holes. He takes it away; and by doing so (and in this context we can remove the physical being of man from our considerations) he enters into a certain relationship with the soul-world and then also with the spirit-land, as you find described in *Theosophy*. He has this relationship through having these elements within him. During physical life, however, they are bound up with the physical body; and then they become free. Through their becoming free, everything is gradually transformed. During physical life the feelers (see the left, dark-shaded part of Diagram 4—I have now removed the differentiations and am drawing the soul-life in this simplified way) are extended into our holes; after death they are withdrawn. But through the feelers being withdrawn, the soul-life itself is hollowed out and the life of the spirit emerges within the soul-life; the spiritual life is absorbed from the other side [light shaded area].

Diagram 4

To the same extent that a person ceases to be immersed in the physical body the soul-spiritual aspect of his being lights up, filling his aura with light from the other side. And just as he is able to attain consciousness as a result of the reflection caused by the continual impact of his soul-spiritual being upon his physical body, so does he now acquire a consciousness by drawing back against the light. But this is that first light of the Sun which is associated with the good. So whereas during his physical life man as a soul-spiritual being pushes against what is related to the Sun, namely against the more-than-empty holes in the brain, when he withdraws after death he encounters the other Sun, the good Sun, the first Sun.

You see how the possibility of acquiring concepts of the life between death and a new birth is bound up with the fundamental ideas of the ancient mysteries; for we are to such a degree placed within the whole of the cosmic life that I have been speaking to you about in the course of these days. But in order to arrive at true concepts of these matters one needs to enter more deeply into the whole structure of human evolution during the earthly age. It could after all be possible that through a particular stroke of good fortune, as one might call it, someone would have a clairvoyant perception of the whole of what I have been describing. But the stroke of good fortune could not lead beyond seeing ever-changing images. One could put it roughly like this. Let us suppose that through some kind of miracle (although these things do not happen miraculously), thus through some sort of clairvoyant, supersensible experience, someone were to see man's life of soul and spirit in a similar way to how I have been trying to portray it here. You will find that it makes sense that this should look rather different from what I was describing a short time ago as the normal aura if you understand that a few days ago [see Lecture 2, Diagram 2] I was describing the aura that results when one sees the whole person, thus the physical human being and the aura that surrounds him; whereas I have now taken out the soul and spiritual aspect of man's being, so that this aspect is abstracted from the physical aspect.

From this you can see that one sometimes needs to arrange the colours one way and sometimes in another way; and you can also see that for a supersensible consciousness things look very different. Set yourself the task of simply seeing the human aura as it is while a person is in the physical body, then look at this aura; turn your attention, therefore, from man as a soul-spiritual being and try to see someone who merely extends his organs into the physical aspect of man. But when you see a person in the time between death and a new birth, you again see how everything is transformed. In particular, this region that I have drawn red here [Diagram 3] goes away from where it is and goes up here, the yellow goes down here, and the whole picture gradually becomes confused. One can perceive such things, but it becomes confusing to look at them. This is why it will not be easy for people today to find a way of bringing sense and meaning to this confusion, unless they resort to other means of assistance.

We have indicated that the human head points towards the past, while the extremities point towards the future. It is a total contrast, a polar opposite situation. Whereas (if you recall what I said yesterday) the head and the extremities are actually one and the same, the head is a very old formation, it is over-formed. That is why it has the holes. There are no holes in the extremities, which are not as yet completely filled with matter. To have these holes is a sign of overdevelopment. A backward-looking development can be seen in the head, and much depends on that. Much also depends on understanding that the extremities are a youthful metamorphosis, whereas the head is an old metamorphosis. And because the extremities represent a youthful metamorphosis, they are unable as yet to think here in physical life but are deeply unconscious. They do not open up such holes to the soul-spiritual aspect of man's being as does the brain.

This is of infinite importance and will in future become more and more important for intellectual and cultural life: to understand that two things which are in an outward, physical sense as completely different from one another as are the head and the extremities are in a soul-spiritual sense one and the same, although at different stages of development in time. Many mysteries lie in this fact that two physically diverse things can actually be one and the same thing at temporally different stages of development. From an outward physical point of view they are quite different, but they are developmental states, or metamorphoses of the same thing.

Goethe's theory of metamorphosis[3] represents an initial attempt to clothe something of this nature with concepts. Whereas the development of appropriate concepts had come to a standstill since ancient times, this faculty re-emerged with Goethe. These concepts are the living concepts of metamorphosis. Goethe began with the simplest things. He said[4] that if we look at a plant we see its green leaves; but they are transformed into the coloured petals of the flower. Both are the same; they are merely metamorphoses of one another. Just as the green leaf of the plant and the red rose petal are metamorphoses of one another, the same thing at different stages, man's head and his extremities too are simply metamorphoses of each other. If we consider Goethe's idea of the metamorphosis of the plant, we have something primitive, simple; but this idea can bring to fruition one of great sublimity, in that it can serve to describe the transition that a human being makes from one incarnation to another. We see a plant with its green leaves and its blossom and say: the blossom, the red rose blossom has arisen from the green leaf. We see a human being standing before us and say: the head that you bear represents your transformed arms, hands, legs and feet from your previous incarnation; and the arms, hands, legs and feet that you have now will be transformed into your head for your next incarnation.

But now there comes an objection which clearly weighs heavily upon you. You will say: But surely I am going to leave my legs and feet behind, and my arms and hands as well; I am certainly not taking them with me into my next incarnation! How will my head develop out of them? This objection is perfectly understandable. But you would again be clinging to maya. It is, you see, not true that you actually leave your legs and your feet, your hands and your arms behind. This is not really so; you say this because you are clinging to maya, to the great illusion. What you ordinarily call your arms and hands, your legs and feet are not your arms and hands and your legs and feet but, rather, the blood and other fluids that are filling your arms and hands and your legs and feet. This is a difficult idea to take hold of, but it is true. We do indeed have arms and hands, legs and feet; but what we have here is of a spiritual nature, they are spiritual forces. You need to realize that your arms and hands, your legs and feet are forces—supersensible forces. If you only had these forces you would not see them with your eyes. They have been filled out, these forces have been filled out with fluids, with blood; and what you see as mineral substance, which is largely fluid in nature and only to the smallest degree solid, fills out these invisible forces [hatching in Diagram 5]. What you leave in the grave or what is burnt are merely what might be called the mineral inclusions. Your arms and hands, your

Diagram 5

legs and feet are not visible feet and so forth, they are forces, and you take them with you. You take the forms with you. You say: I have hands and feet. Someone who perceives the spiritual worlds does not say I have hands and feet; rather does he say that there are Spirits of Form, Elohim, who have cosmic thoughts, and their thoughts are my arms and hands and legs and feet; and their thoughts are filled out with blood and other fluids. But again, blood and other fluids are likewise not what they appear to be physically; these substances are the ideas of the Spirits of Wisdom, and what the physicist calls matter is merely the outer semblance. When the physicist conceives of matter, he should say: here I am encountering a thought of the Spirits of Wisdom, the Kyriotetes. And when you see arms and hands, legs and feet, which you cannot really even touch, you should say: Here the cosmic thoughts of the Spirits of Form are shaping my bodily forms.

In short, however strange it may seem, there are no such things as your bodies, but where your body is in space the cosmic thoughts of the higher hierarchies are intermingled. And if you were to see rightly instead of in accordance with maya, you would say that the cosmic thoughts of the Exusiai, the Spirits of Form, the Elohim, are projecting into it. These cosmic thoughts make themselves visible to me through being filled out with the cosmic thoughts of the Spirits of Wisdom. That gives us arms and hands, legs and feet. Nothing whatsoever can be beheld by spiritual vision in the way that it appears in maya; there are only cosmic thoughts, and these cosmic thoughts gather together and are condensed, are thrust against one another, with the result that they appear to us as these shadowy figures in whose form we walk around, believing that they are real. Thus physical man does not exist at all.

We can say with a certain qualification that in the hour of death the Spirits of Form separate their cosmic thoughts from the cosmic thoughts of the Spirits of Wisdom. The Spirits of Form take their thoughts up into the air, the Spirits of Wisdom lower their material thoughts into the Earth. Because of this there is in the corpse a shadowy legacy of the thoughts of the Spirits of Wisdom when the Spirits of Form have taken their thoughts back into the air. This is physical death; this is what it really is.

In short, when we begin to think about reality we arrive at the dissolution of what we ordinarily call the physical world. For this physical world derives its existence from an active interweaving of the thoughts of the spirits of the higher hierarchies with one another. I would therefore ask you to imagine that finely distributed particles of water are being interspersed, forming a thick mist. That is also why your body has such a shadowy aspect, because the thoughts of the Spirits of Form are penetrating those of the Spirits of Wisdom, the formative thoughts are pervading the thoughts of substance. When viewed in this way the whole world dissolves into a spiritual perspective. But it is important to be able to conceive of the world in a truly spiritual way, to know that it is only apparent that my arms and hands, my feet and legs are given over to the Earth. The truth of the matter is that the meta-morphosis of my arms and legs, hands and feet is beginning there and will be completed in the life between death and a new birth, and my arms and legs, hands and feet will become my head in my next incar-nation.

Much of what I have been saying now may, at any rate in the way that it has been expressed, have struck you as somewhat strange. But what have we ultimately been saying if it is not that we are ascending from a semblance of man to true man, from what lives outwardly in maya to the successive ranks of the hierarchies? Only if one does this can one speak in a mature way today of man's potential to acquire knowledge of a so-called higher self. If one merely makes declarations about the higher self, if one simply says: I feel a higher self within me, it has no substance; for the ordinary self belongs to maya, and is therefore itself maya—the higher self has meaning only if one speaks of it in relation to the world of the higher hierarchies. To speak of the higher self without taking account of the world that consists of the Spirits of Form and the Angels, Archangels and so forth, to speak of the higher self without reference to this world, signifies that one is speaking in empty abstractions; and it also means that one is not speaking of what lives in man between death and a new birth. For just as we live here with animals, plants and minerals, so do we live between death and a new birth with the kingdoms of the higher hierarchies, of whom we have often spoken. Only when we gradually come nearer to these ideas and concepts (which will not be possible for another week or so)[5] will we be able to approach an answer to the question: why do many people die as young children, many in old age and others somewhere in between?

What I have now described to you in outline are concrete concepts for the realities of the world. They are indeed not abstract concepts that I have been presenting to you, they are concrete concepts of world realities. Such concepts as these existed in the ancient mysteries, albeit for a more atavistic perception. Since the eighth century BC they have been lost to human perception; and they must be rediscovered through a deepening of our comprehension of the Christ Being. This can only happen on a path of inner, spiritual-scientific research.

Let us once more form for ourselves a kind of overview of human evolution from a particular standpoint. The concepts that we are now wanting to grasp are extremely important. It can be said that if one looks back over human evolution one comes to see—as I have often described—that in olden times people had more of the group-soul nature and that individual souls were initially members of such a group soul. You can read about this in various cycles.[6] One could accordingly portray human evolution diagrammatically by saying that in former times there were group souls, and each of these group souls split up (this is how it would appear to a purely soul-based perception; for a spiritual perception it would be somewhat different). Each of these souls is then clothed with a body, which I am indicating here with red lines [see Diagram 6].

Diagram 6

Until the time of the Pythagorean School people would make drawings of this sort, and they would say: look at your bodies, human beings are separated as regards their bodies, each one has his own body (that is why the red lines are isolated from one another); but as far as souls are concerned mankind is a unity, in that we go back in the dim distant past to the group soul. There we have a unity. If you think away the red, the lightly shaded part of the drawing forms a unified figure.

However, it only makes sense to speak about this figure if one has first spoken about the spiritual aspect of man's being as we have today; for then we know everything that is exerting an influence on these souls, how the higher hierarchies are actively working within them. There is no sense in speaking about this figure if one does not have the hierarchies clearly in mind. People spoke in this way right up to the time of the Pythagorean School, and it was from the Pythagorean School that Apollonius learnt what I spoke about yesterday and about which I shall be speaking further next week. But since the eighth century BC (and the Pythagorean Schools were a kind of last bastion in this respect), the possibility of speaking in this way has been lost. And the concepts which, through being related to the higher hierarchies have an intrinsic reality, have become vague and confused for people. Thus instead of the world of the Angels, Archangels, Archai, Spirits of Form, Spirits of Movement, Spirits of Wisdom and Thrones, instead of all this clearly defined weaving of the spirit they arrived at a concept which came to play a certain part in the perception of the Greeks—that of pneuma, in which everything is intermingled. Pneuma, spirit in general—this vague concept which pantheists still love today: spirit, spirit, spirit, spirit! I have often spoken of how pantheists place spirit everywhere. But this goes back to the Greeks. This figure is again being portrayed; but you can now see that what was formerly an intrinsic reality—the fullness of the Godhead—has become an abstract concept, pneuma. The white, or light-shaded, areas are pneuma, the rest is physical matter [see Diagram 6], if one is considering the evolution of mankind. But the Greeks still at least perceived this pneuma, for they saw something of the aura; so that what they pictured in the white or light-shaded branches had an auric quality and was therefore actually perceptible. This is the great significance of the transition from Greece to Rome, that the Greeks still perceived pneuma as something truly spiritual but that the Romans did so no longer. With the Romans everything became completely abstract, a total abstraction, mere concepts. The Romans are the people of abstract concepts.

My dear friends, in modern times you find the same diagram in science! You can encounter it today in materialistic books on science—there you find exactly the same diagram that you would have found in the old mysteries, in the Pythagorean Schools, where everything was still related to the hierarchies. You find it in the Greeks, where it was related to pneuma; you find people drawing it again today. We shall see what it has become today. Today the scientist says to his students as he draws this same drawing on the blackboard: in the reproductive process of the human race the germinal substance of the parents is passed on to the children; but part of this substance remains so that in the next generation it can again be passed on to the children, and likewise a part of this remains so that it can once again be passed on to the children, while another part of the germinal substance forms the cells of the physical body. You have exactly the same diagram except that the modern scientist sees in the white or light-shaded area [see Diagram 6] the continuity of the germinal substance. He says: if we go back to our human ancestors and identify their germinal substance, the germinal substance of both male and female, and then go to people today and do the same with them, it is a single stream, the substance is continuous. Something eternal always remains in the germinal substance—so the scientist imagines—and only something like half of the germinal plasma is passed on to the new body. The scientist again has the same figure, but now he no longer has the pneuma; and the white or light-shaded area is the material germinal substance. There is no longer anything of a soul and spiritual nature, it is just material substance. You can read this in what modern scientists write, and it is considered today to be a discovery of great significance. This is the materializing of a lofty spiritual idea, in that it has undergone a process of abstraction; it has an abstract concept at its centre. It is amusing to think that a modern scientist has written a book (at least, it is amusing to anyone who can think properly) in which he clearly says: what the Greeks still conceived of as pneuma is today's germinal substance with its continuity of existence. Yes, it is a foolish thing to say; but it is considered to be great wisdom today.

One thing is, however, clear from this: it is not the drawing that matters! You will therefore understand why I was never very keen on drawing diagrams while we were still trying to implement anthroposophy through the Theosophical Society. One only had to enter any theosophical branch and one would find the walls plastered with all manner of such diagrams. There were drawings of every conceivable thing, together with descriptive texts; there were whole genealogical trees and sketches of everything imaginable. But what matters is not these drawings; what really counts is that one can really arrive at a living imagination. For the drawing can be exactly the same whether you conceive of it in a soul-spiritual way as the manifestation of the hierarchies or whether you are thinking of something purely material, the continuing existence of germinal plasma. People today are very hazy about such things. This is why it is so important to be clear that the Greeks still knew something about man's real self, about spiritual reality, and that the Romans made the transition to abstract concepts. You can see this in purely outward details. When the Greeks speak about their gods, they speak in such a way that one sees very precisely that they are imagining quite specific figures behind these deities. For the Romans the Gods are actually only names, only labels; they are abstractions and become ever more so. For the Greeks there was still a certain notion that in the person standing before one the hierarchies are living, and that the hierarchies live differently in each individual. The Greeks related to others in accordance with their reality, and when they said, 'This is Alcibiades, this is Socrates, this is Plato,' they still had the concept that in Alcibiades, in Socrates, in Plato the cosmic thoughts of the hierarchies are being manifested in a variety of ways, and that it is because of this that such different figures appear.

This was lost with the Romans. They therefore formed a system of concepts which had its most extreme expression in that from Augustus[7] onwards—and actually from somewhat earlier—the Roman Caesar was considered to be God. The Godhead gradually became an abstraction; the Roman Caesar was himself a God because this concept [of God] had become completely abstract. But their other concepts also became abstract. This was especially the case with the legal and moral concepts that pervaded the Roman nature, with the result that a whole mountain of abstractions came to replace the ancient heritage of living thoughts. And all these abstractions remained as a legacy throughout the Middle Ages and were bequeathed to modern times, bringing this legacy down to the nineteenth century—abstract concepts that are carried into every sphere.

In the nineteenth century something rather startling happened. Man completely disappeared amongst these abstract concepts. The Greeks still had an inkling of man's true being, which is fashioned from out of the cosmos; in the course of the Roman era man's being became obscured. It was necessary for the nineteenth century to rediscover him amidst all the circumstances to which I have already referred and regarding which I shall speak in greater detail. This discovery of man now emerged from a different pole. The Greeks had sought to view man as the divine human being who originates from the hierarchies; the Romans had replaced this with a series of abstract concepts. The task of the nineteenth century—and also to some extent the eighteenth century, but particularly the nineteenth—was to rediscover man from a different aspect, from the animal side of his nature. However, he could not be understood in this way with these abstract concepts. This was the great shock. And that is the great shock, the deep cleft that arises. What is this that stands before us on two legs and fidgets with its hands and eats and drinks all kinds of things? What is it? The Greeks still knew the answer; but then this answer was changed into abstract concepts. Now it startles people in the nineteenth century; there it is, but people have no concepts to grasp it with. They conceive of it as merely a higher animal; on the one hand, from the scientific aspect, there is Darwinism and on the other hand, from the aspect of the world of ideas, socialism, which would endeavour to view man's place in society as that of an animal. So we have man confronting himself in a state of bewilderment. What is this I see? And he is powerless to answer this question.

That is the situation today, this is the situation which will not only give rise to concepts that are true or false, as people find appropriate, but also brings with it the challenge to accomplish deeds that will be either catastrophic or beneficial in their outcome. This, then, is the situation: the shock that a person has on confronting himself. It has once again become essential to find the elements necessary for the understanding of man as a spiritual being. These elements will not be found unless one turns to the theory of metamorphosis. That is the essential point. Only Goethe's concepts of metamorphosis are able to comprehend the ever-changing phenomena which present themselves to a perception of reality.

It would be true to say that the cultural evolution of humanity has always been proceeding in this direction. Even at the time when *The Chymical Wedding* and other writings were being published in so wonderful a way in the seventeenth century (as I have indicated in *Das Reich* in a series of articles on *The Chymical Wedding of Christian Rosenkreutz*[8]), there was already the endeavour to ensure that a social structure compatible with man's true nature should come into being. It was in this way that *The Chymical Wedding of Christian Rosenkreutz* by the so-called Valentin Andreae[9] came to be written. But on the other hand there also emerged the book which he called *Allgemeine Reformation der ganzen weiten Welt* ('General Reformation of the Whole Wide World'),[10] where he gives an extensive political survey of how social conditions might come to be. But all this was swept away by the Thirty Years War.

At that time it was the Thirty Years War that swept it all away. Today it is possible either for the world situation to sweep all this away again or to adopt it as part of human evolution. With this we are touching upon the great fundamental question of the present time, a question that people should be concerning themselves with in preference to all the secondary questions that preoccupy them today. If people were to concern themselves with this basic question, they would find ways and means of bringing fruitful ideas to bear upon present-day realities; and this would be a way of getting away from abstract concepts.

It is not so easy to distinguish reality from illusion. In these circumstances one really needs to want to enter into life with all seriousness and good will instead of being content with programmes and prejudices. I could give you lots of examples of this kind of phenomenon, but I shall cite just one instance. At the beginning of the 1890s a number of people came together in several different towns or cities in Europe and imitated something in the American style, namely the 'Movement for Ethical Culture'.[11] The impulse for founding these 'societies for ethical culture' emanated at that time from certain intellectuals. These people produced some very beautiful things, and if you read today the articles that were written then by these representatives of the 'societies for ethical culture'—if you have a taste for such rich and refined fare—you will probably still be able to take delight in all the beautiful ideals in which these people were indulging at that time. And it was indeed no pleasant task to take issue with this wallowing in such rich and refined ideals. However, I wrote an article[12] in one of the first numbers of the journal *Die Zukunft* ('The Future')[13] that was critical of this oily indulgence of 'ethical culture' and indeed had a massive grumble about it. It was of course a shameful thing to do, for it was indeed somewhat shameful to cast negative aspersions upon something so worthy, when these people were, after all, aiming to make the whole world ethical and moral! I was living at the time in Weimar but when paying a visit to Berlin I spoke with Herman Grimm,[14] who said: 'What is your problem with this "ethical culture"? Approach the people themselves and you will see that those who are coming together here in Berlin to speak about ethics are really nice, kind people. One really cannot have any problem with them. They are people who can be really nice to know, who one can come to like very well.' None of this could be denied, and at the time Herman Grimm was no less right than I was. Outwardly, one of us was just as right at that particular moment as the other, the case of each of us could be proved just as well as the other's; and I would not want to maintain that from a purely logical point of view my issues with these ethical philosophers were more justified than those brought forward by them. But it is from this over-refined idealism that the present catastrophe has arisen, and the only people who were right and have been justified by events are those who said at that time: with all your indulgent talk about high-faluting ideals, through which you want to bring universal peace, universal morality and other such aims to humanity, you have given rise to nothing other than what I have called the social carcinoma[15] that in the end led inevitably to the present catastrophe. Time has shown who has been working with real concepts and who has been working with mere abstractions. When concepts are purely abstract in character it is impossible to decide whether someone is right or wrong; the only decisive factor is whether or not an idea finds its rightful place in the course of events. When a professor is teaching science at a university, he can of course give beautiful and logical proofs that everything that he is saying is correct. All this goes right into the holes of the head (and on this occasion I mean this in the best sense). But you see, the question is not whether any apparently good logical grounds can be given but that the same thoughts, when they enter a head such as Lenin's,[16] become Bolshevism. What matters is what a thought becomes in reality. It is of no importance what one can think about it or what one can feel about it in an abstract sense but what power is forming a thought in its actual reality. And if one is evaluating that world view that most people have been speaking about recently (because the others have been preoccupied with aesthetics), namely socialism, it is not now a question of getting down to swotting up on Karl Marx[17] or Lassalle[18] or Bernstein[19] (in other words, studying their books, studying these writers) but of having a feeling, a living experience for what will happen in the further progress of mankind if a number of people—the sort of people who stand at machines—have these thoughts. This is what matters, rather than having ideas about the social structure in the near future that are taught in the accepted course of diplomatic training. Now is the time when what matters is to be able to weigh up thoughts so as to be able to answer the question: what is wanted by the times in the coming decades? The time has now already come when it is not enough to sit in comfort on a variety of magisterial chairs[20] and quietly continue cherishing old habits. It is now time when people must experience the shock of confronting themselves, when the thought needs to arise in those who are responsible anywhere for anything: how is this question to be solved out of the inner* life? We shall speak further about this next time.

---

* The German word used here is *geistig*—Translator.

Lecture 7

I have recently been presenting here a number of important facts about man which can be investigated in a spiritual-scientific way. I attach less importance to whether the details of these facts are understood (as I have often spoken about matters of this nature); my concern is, rather, that a certain impression should be awakened through what I have put forward, an impression of the nature of what can be referred to as the illusion of the outer physical world. I want you to acquire a feeling for what is actually meant when the outer world as we see it around us— and I specifically say 'see' rather than 'have'—is spoken of initially as an illusion, while behind it lies the true or real world. I have also been wanting to evoke a deeper feeling for what is meant when one is speaking of the real world on the foundation of spiritual science. So we have been dealing mainly with these general feelings. In this regard I have arrived at that point where in a certain sense we have an opportunity to link our spiritual-scientific observations with significant matters of concern in the cultural life of the present time (and I am thinking here of a wider perspective, not just our immediate present but the centuries in which we are living).

There is a dichotomy in our cultural life which one can characterize in many different ways and also define in more than one way. However, all these definitions must ultimately coalesce in two streams that we have to visualize as streams of thought emanating from the intellectual life of the present which do not properly come together. One of these two streams of thought can be referred to in the broadest sense as the scientific stream, and by this I do not only mean what is thought and asserted in scientific circles but the scientific stream as it lives today in the feeling life of more or less the whole of mankind. This scientific stream has gradually become a popular and very widespread outlook on life, and it has produced concepts that have taken deep root in the inner life of people today. One can most clearly see how this scientific view of the world has taken root if one observes that it has become most deeply entrenched where people believe that they are reaching towards the life of the spirit. Ultimately, what is commonly known as spiritualism, which very many people consider to be theosophical theories, is nothing other than an outcome of a materialistic view of the world. The concepts that are engendered for the most part about the ether and astral bodies, together with what is arrived at by means of experiments in spiritualistic séances, are wholly clothed in concepts borrowed from the scientific world view, as is made most evident by people like du Prel, for instance,[1] who believes that he is about to enter the spiritual world. But everything that he says about the spiritual world is formulated in scientific concepts, that is, in concepts that are only appropriate for thinking about nature, not about the spirit. Similarly, it is striking how materialistic the theories of most theosophists are, and how great an effort they make to relate notions such as the ether body or even the astral body to scientific concepts which should only be applied to nature. The ether body is very often conceived of as something of a wholly material nature, as a fine mist or something of the sort. Well, I have often expressed my view about these matters.

This is the one category of concepts that we have in our time—those of natural science. So that I am not misunderstood, I shall emphasize once again that it is of less significance that these scientific concepts are to be found in the sciences themselves, where they are largely justified; the important point is that they are used where there is a wish to understand matters of an inner, spiritual nature. Many people even live in the illusion that they are saying something special if they stress the similarity of the concepts that they use in this spiritual domain with those of natural science.

The significant fact that we need to keep in mind is that these scientific concepts can only embrace a certain sphere of our world, a certain sphere of the world in which we are living, that another world must remain outside our consciousness if we employ only scientific concepts. Thus these scientific concepts form the one stream.

The other stream is composed of certain concepts that we form for ourselves about ideas or ideals; and the whole theme of morality has also for quite some time been part of this stream. Take a scientific idea such as heredity or evolution. You are thinking scientifically if you think through such an idea clearly and concisely; but if you extend these ideas of heredity and evolution as they are generally understood by science into the domain of the spirit, your mind becomes confused. Consider certain concepts that one needs in life, such as the inner freedom of our soul, good will, moral perfection, or higher concepts of a loftier nature such as love, you have again a stream of ideas, of concepts, which are likewise justified because they are used in daily life. But one would be deluding oneself if one were to try to build a bridge between the way that people think scientifically today and the way that ideals, ideas and moral impulses are conceived of in our time. When someone is thinking in a purely scientific way, that is, when he is seeking a world outlook that accords with natural science (which is the ideal cherished by many people today), there is no place in a world that corresponds to this world outlook for all that is understood by notions such as good will or even, for example, happiness, love and inner freedom. The scientific way of thinking has the specific aim of bringing everything into the orbit of the concept of causality, of thinking of everything in terms of cause and effect. A favourite generalization to which I have often referred[2] is the law of the conservation of energy and matter. If you imagine an outlook on the world where only the scientific concepts of cause and effect or the conservation of energy and matter have any validity, you would—unless you were to be insincere in the way you view the world—have to say that in a world order where only such laws apply everything that has to do with ideals, ideas and moral concepts really becomes nothing more than a joke. For a view of the world where the law of the conservation of energy and matter is a universal truth, it makes no sense to say anything except that our world order evolves in accordance with the law of the conservation of energy and matter, and that, moreover, the human race has also arisen within this world order from certain causes. This human race dreams of good will, love, inner freedom; but these are all ideas that people form for themselves, and once those conditions have arisen in our world system that must indeed arise according to the ideas of modern science this means that all notions such as good will, inner freedom and love can be well and truly buried. These are dreams that people dream while fulfilling their lives within earthly evolution in accordance with purely natural laws, and it is therefore meaningless to say anything with regard to the worth of ideals and ideas other than that they are dreams that people dream; for in such a scientific world view ideas and ideals lack the power to become realities. So once the situation has arisen that one must necessarily envisage if one thinks in terms of scientific concepts, what will become of ideas and ideals will have to be buried! However, the way that people conceive of ideas and ideals today is such that—even though they do not acknowledge it—their ideas lack the inner strength to be transformed into realities. They are simply mere thoughts which achieve realization through people attaching their feelings to them and behaving towards one another in a way that corresponds to the ideas. But they have no inner power to become realities, in the way that magnetism, electricity or heat have; for these qualities possess the inner power to become actual phenomena! Ideas as such—think especially in this regard of moral ideas—do not have this inner power to become realities amidst our modern world conception, if our thoughts are confined to those of natural science.

It is true that only very few people have a clear perspective of the division that exists between these two streams active in our present age, but the division does indeed exist; and the fact that it plays a part in the subconscious regions of man's being is of far greater importance than any theoretical perception of its role. Only *one* layer of man's consciousness has a clear theoretical grasp of what I have just been saying, and one needs to keep an eye on this aspect of human consciousness in present-day life. Clearly stated, this means that the whole world is ordered solely in accordance with scientific laws, and that ideas and ideals have significance only because people have the feeling that they should be guided by them in their behaviour towards one another—a view that one finds at present in the theories of socialism. For this reason socialist theory today rejects any science of the spirit, and even considers the remnants of the ancient spiritual wisdom which are still to be found in jurisprudence, ethics and theology to be prejudices that belong to mankind's infancy and wants everything that one might call spiritual science to be understood as social science; its aim is to present socialist social science as being the only valid path with respect to the mutual relationships of human beings. The world is scientifically ordered, and the only interpretation of the world that can be added to the explanations of natural science is that of social science. This is the fundamental conviction of everyone who is conscious of being a socialist.

If one is wanting to investigate such things properly, one should not allow one's thoughts to become confused. I know of course that people may come and say that socialists do not think like this. But as I said in the first few days when I started lecturing here again, what matters is not the content of the ideas but what enables ideas to become active, how they exert an influence and live in people. The ideas of socialism take hold of people by rejecting all talk of any kind of spiritual world-substance, by maintaining that this world-substance is ordered wholly in accordance with scientific laws and that spiritual science should be replaced by social science alone.

As a result people feel that ideas and ideals, when they are conceived in the way that they are thought in the present, indeed no longer have any power beyond dwelling in their inner lives as a dream that is dreamed by humanity in the course of earthly evolution. No idea, even the most beautiful and idealistic, has the power to enable something to grow, to engender warmth, cause a magnet to move or anything of that kind. It is therefore condemned to be a mere dream, because—for as long as the world order is conceived of as being merely the sum of electrical and magnetic forces, forces of light and heat, and so forth—it cannot affect the structure of these forces, especially when the law of the conservation of energy and matter is proposed, according to which energy and matter are of eternal validity. Ideas are therefore never able to take hold, because energy and matter are always there, they have their own, eternal laws.

Incidentally, these laws of the conservation of energy and matter are the cause of much mischief. When present-day writers refer to the law of the conservation of energy and matter (and especially of energy), they

often say that it originated with Julius Robert Mayer.[3] Anyone who is
really familiar with Julius Robert Mayer's writings will know that it is
just as intelligent to trace the law of the conservation of energy and
matter to Julius Robert Mayer in the way that contemporary writers do
as to ascribe the origins of trashy literature to the invention of the
printing press by Gutenberg.[4] For what does duty in textbooks and
standard manuals as the law of the conservation of energy and matter
has nothing to do with the law of Julius Robert Mayer, who was confined to a lunatic asylum because of what he did.

However, the essential question for anyone who takes spiritual
science seriously is this: what relationship, what connection exists
between these two things which can never be united according to the
present world view, namely moral idealism and a naturalistic perception
of the world? This question cannot be answered theoretically as simply
as that. There is at present a demand for theoretical answers, and those
who take up theosophy or anthroposophy in some way are sometimes
the strongest voices carving theoretical and dogmatic answers. But the
answers that are given on the foundation of spiritual science must be
answers involving perception. In this respect it is not right if one
incorporates the present predilection for dogmatism into spiritual science. Spiritual science demands something different. It is certainly true
that spiritual scientists often demand that different dogmas be put
forward, but spiritual science cannot possibly be of the view that
another set of dogmas should simply replace those already in existence
but that one should both think and perceive in a different way, and that
furthermore certain things should be considered from completely different points of view. What is often practised today either under the
name of spiritual science or of theosophy can frequently give one the
impression of being a somewhat modified form of medieval Scholasticism. I do not want to say anything against Scholasticism, for there are
certain things in Scholasticism that are far more significant than the
philosophical outpourings of our present age. But many people are
currently drawn merely to acquire different dogmas, whether about
God, immortality and heaven knows what else, and thus to think differently but nevertheless only to think rather than arriving at perceptions that have a totally different foundation from previous ideas. If one

is standing firmly on the ground of spiritual science, one will say: at the time of Scholasticism people wove all manner of weird ideas about the Trinity, about the nature of man, about his immortality and about the Christ problem, if the epithet that I have used is understood without any negative overtones; for the essential value of Scholasticism lies not in the dogmas that it put forward but in the technique of thinking, as I have described it in my essay *Philosophy and Anthroposophy* (which has now appeared in a new, and considerably expanded edition),[5] it resides in the way that people thought about things. Nevertheless, it is actually more possible to understand this thinking today if one turns to the Scholastics than to the many confused ideas that are referred to these days as being theological or philosophical. Enough theorizing has been done about these matters in the Middle Ages. There were, for example, many theoretical battles about the problem of the Christ Being. Anyone who knows anything about the nature of these struggles will not acquire a taste for the somewhat varied kind of Scholasticism that one finds, for example, in theosophy, where instead of the Trinity, immortality and whatever else that prevailed in former times one is now presented with physical, etheric and astral bodies. It is a different variety of theorizing, but it is from a qualitative point of view fundamentally the same thing. Anyone who would enter deeply into this medieval Scholasticism knows that it is a futile pursuit to try, shall we say, to gain access to the Mystery of Golgotha by this means. Today it is far more important, for example, to achieve a conception of Christ Jesus, which has been attempted by us here in the Group[6] that is to stand at the focal point of the building, where the aim has been once more to envisage the figure of Christ Jesus. Anyone who is interested in the right way in former dogmas will be far more interested today in drawing the form of Christ forth from spiritual life, because the time has now come for this to be done. The Middle Ages was the time for astute thinking and for working out scholastic concepts to the nth degree; whereas our present time—as I have often said—is a point in the fifth post-Atlantean epoch when the perception of human beings must be directed towards spiritual forms. In former times any depiction of the form of Christ was of an imaginary nature. I have often spoken of the gradual development of these representations.[7] With the means of spiritual perception the figure of Christ can once more be found. Thus every age has its particular task. For what matters is not that things become fixed but that man engages in a quest in his development and works his way through to ever further stages in his evolution.

Hence the important thing is that a bridge can be found where the modern world outlook is unable to find one and where—if it is inwardly consistent—it is inevitably led to socialism, that is, to socialist theory. And, as I have often said, this is not socialism in its justified form. The bridge will, however, only be found if one earnestly has the will to enter just as much into what takes place between death and a new birth as one does into what elapses between birth and death—if, therefore, one not merely endeavours to analyse the physical world but truly has the will to venture into the spiritual world. One speaks about man and says that he consists of physical body, ether body, astral body and ego, and so on. This is certainly justified, but only for the human being as he lives here on Earth between birth and death. But what I explained here last time and the time before can already make it clear to you that one can speak in a similar way about man's state of being after death, between death and a new birth. If you were to ask what constitutes the being of man, it is not adequate to relate this question merely to his earthly being but we must now also pose the question: what does he consist of when he is not on Earth but in a spiritual world between death and a new birth? In what way can one then speak of the various members of man's being? It must be possible to speak of them in no less real a way. And if one really thinks about such a question with complete honesty one becomes clearly aware of the fact that every age has its particular task.

People do not fully realize that the way that they think, imagine and even feel and, indeed, perceive the outer world belongs very much to our present time (you need only to recall certain elucidations that I gave in my *Riddles of Philosophy*[8] concerning the relatively short period of time from 600 BC until now). We cannot go back beyond the eighth century before the Mystery of Golgotha with the thinking, feeling and perception that we have now. I have given you the precise year: 747 before the Mystery of Golgotha is the date of the founding of the city of Rome. If one goes beyond this pre-Christian century, the whole manner of human life is different to the inner life characteristic of today. All ways of perceiving the world were different then. This is clearly a boundary that is easier to distinguish than the other one which is also very evident, though not as yet for people today: the boundary that lies in the fifteenth century. The fifteenth century is too close to people today; they cannot acquire any real insight into the great transition that occurred then. They generally imagine that thinking and perceiving have always had a similar character to the way they are now, however far back one goes—and yet one doesn't have to go back very far! And the fact is that as soon as one goes back beyond the eighth century BC one is confronted by a completely different kind of thinking. So we can now pose the question: why was it necessary for there to be a different kind of thinking? When people today form ideas about this different way of thinking their notions are rather foolish, if I may say so. Thus when present-day human beings hear how teaching was carried out in, for example, the Egyptian mysteries (which were the most sought-after at that time), when they hear about the way that truths were discussed there, they say to themselves: well, that accords perfectly with the fantasies of that time, when people weren't so clever as they are now and they still had childish ideas about things. It is only now that we see them as they really are! There is a particularly strong tendency to think in this way today, for when one has become so embroiled in present-day thinking it is impossible to have a different view of anything. Let us suppose that a Greek—for example, Pythagoras[9]—had gone to Egypt and had studied there, just as someone might go to a famous university today in order to study. What would he have learnt? I shall tell you what Pythagoras was really able to learn there. He learnt that in ancient times Mercury played chess with the Moon,[10] and that Mercury was victorious in this game of chess. He won 20 minutes from the Moon for each day, and these 20 minutes were then counted up by the initiates. How much do these 20 minutes add up to over 360 days? They come to five days exactly. So a year was reckoned to have not 360 days but 365 days. These five days are the ones that Mercury won from the Moon in the game and which he then presented to the other planets and to the human race as an addition to the 360 days that the year already had.

Well, if one says that Pythagoras was able to learn something of this sort from the wise Egyptians, anyone now will naturally have a good laugh. Nevertheless, this is merely a different way of expressing a deep spiritual truth—and we will speak further about this in the course of these days—which our present age has not rediscovered but is none the less true.

You might well ask why these calculations were formerly done in a different way. Compare what such an Egyptian sage[11] tells his newly enlisted pupil Pythagoras about Mercury having won 20 minutes per day from the Moon in a game of chess with a lecture about modern astronomy in an auditorium and you will have a better idea of the contrast. But if one asks why there is such a difference, one needs to go more deeply into the whole essence of human evolution. For if one goes back before the eighth century BC (it is true that Pythagoras does not belong to this early time, but in Egypt there were still remnants of a wisdom that had its origin long before the eighth century BC which was able to make its influence felt) and one finds a teaching of this nature there will be a good reason for this. Man's whole relationship to the world was viewed differently, and this had to be so at that time.

I should like to point out that it has happened time and again that various remnants of ancient seership have been atavistically renewed—and by the word 'atavistic' I do not have anything disparaging in mind. Anyone who, for example, reads a book such as Jakob Böhme's *De Signatura Rerum* will say, if he is honest, that he does not know what to make of it. For some quite remarkable statements are made here that must either be evaluated from a higher standpoint (when they will begin to make sense) or, from the point of view of a modern thinking person, be rejected as the irrational testimony of a layman who is a bit crazy. All the absurd things that are said amongst immature groups of theosophists about Jakob Böhme[12] have an evil, malicious quality. Despite all this talk, in the spiritual structure of his work and in the way that he analyses certain words (when, for example, he divides up words such as sulphur and finds something in its different parts—and we are not concerning ourselves with the substance of what he is saying but with the way that he says it in his book *De Signatura Rerum*), Jakob Böhme recalls far more than we find evidence of in any of the abstract sciences that are currently in the public eye regarding man's actual relationship to the spiritual world in its entirety. Such a man as Jakob

Böhme has a far more intimate connection with the spiritual world. And it is characteristic of such thinkers who were active before the eighth century BC to have such an intimate connection. They did not think with the detached individual intelligence with which we think today. We all think with this detached individual intelligence; they still thought with a cosmic reasoning power, with a creative intelligence which, I may say, one needs to discern in certain of their works if one is to grasp what they are saying.

There is today really only one realm where one can observe to a small degree the way in which something akin to a creative intelligence interweaves and interacts in the life of human beings. In this one realm one can observe something of a self-realization of a non-material dimension; but I must add that there is no more than a shadow of it, and even this shadow is for the most part not really taken into account. There exist today a whole number of naturalistic anthropological theories about the emergence of language and the way that it has been said to evolve. As I have often indicated, there are—as you may remember—two main theories. One of these is called the 'bow-wow' theory and the other the 'ding dong' theory. The bow-wow theory derives more from continental scholars, the ding-dong theory originates from Max Müller.[13] The basis of the bow-wow theory is that human beings emerged from the most primitive conditions and expressed their inner organic experiences like the barking of a dog when it makes the sound bow-wow; and as a result of a corresponding evolution—after all, everything evolves from a primitive to a more perfect stage—the dog's bow-wow, which can still be observed in human beings who are at a primitive stage of development, became human speech. If you trace everything in evolutionary development from bow-wow to modern speech, just as the evolutionary theories of Darwin[14] or Haeckel[15] begin with the simplest monad, that is, with the simplest, most inarticulate form, one arrives at the languages of today. Another theory asserts that one can develop a certain feeling from a relationship with the tolling of a bell, its 'ding-dong' sound; every time one hears it one has the inner experience of a sound that one imitates. Thus the bow-bow contingent is more in tune with the theory of evolution, whereas the ding-dong idea is, rather, a theory of adaptation on the part of man to the inner nature of the material world.* It is then also possible to make ingenious connections between the bow-wow theory and the ding-dong theory, and one arrives at a more complete picture by linking evolution with adaptation. After all, this is more or less the accepted way of viewing such matters. There are also those who ridicule both theories and have others of their own; but these are actually not so very different in principle.

From a spiritual standpoint there can be no question whatsoever of the evolution of language having unfolded in this way. On the contrary, even the outward structure of language already indicates that a real intelligence is at work in the formation of speech and in the arising of language. Indeed, it is interesting to discern the sovereign power of reason specifically in connection with language for the simple reason that in language the driving force of ideas—and, hence, what can be perceived today in the one stream—is most clearly apparent, and also because language is not merely addressed to a person's feelings but has its own structure, with the result that the non-material world comes to expression through it in a certain way, albeit imperfectly when compared with natural laws. Take as an example a particular word—I should like to draw your attention to a few very elementary instances—where you can see how an inner intelligence holds sway in the arising of language. Take a word such as *oratio*—oration or discourse. It is remarkable that, if one takes a word such as *oratio* and then observes what becomes of this word in a person's life after death, an extraordinary similarity emerges with the way that an evolving intelligence has influenced the development of language. This gives one a certain assurance that is difficult to arrive at in another way, for on other paths one can at best achieve only suppositions. A dead person will seldom be able to understand the word *oratio*, at any rate once a certain time has elapsed after death; he will no longer understand it, he loses all com-

---

* The German text based on the original shorthand report here gives the word *Worte* (words)—but even with a fairly liberal way of rendering the phrase as 'the inner nature of outward, physical words' this does not make a great deal of sense to the present translator. If *Welt* is substituted for *Worte* (and neither the shorthand reports nor the published editions based on them are totally free from errors), the meaning inherent in the passage lights up in a far more lucid way.

prehension of it. On the other hand he will still understand a perception or an imagination that can be expressed through the words *os, oris* (mouth) and ratio (reason or intelligence). The dead person breaks up the word *oratio* into *os* and *ratio*. The opposite process took place in the development of the word; for the word *oratio* actually arose as a result of a synthesis of the primary words *os* and *ratio*. *Oratio* is not a primary word like *os, oris* and *ratio* but is formed from *os* and *ratio*.

I want in this way to bring a few such elementary instances to your attention. These things can be studied most clearly in the Latin language, for the reason that they are most distinctly visible there. However, the laws that one can discover are of significance for other languages as well. Take, for example, three primary words: *Ne ego otior* (which as a statement means 'I am not idle'). *Ego otior*, I am idle; *ne ego otior*, I am not idle. These three words are combined together through the cosmic intelligence that governs them in the word *negotior*, which means to trade or negotiate. Three words have thereby joined together into one, and you can see an intelligence in the construction of words, intelligence in the development of language.

As I have said, I would not make such a point of this were it not for the remarkable fact that a dead person takes apart what has in the above way been joined together. The dead person separates a word such as *negotior* into *ne ego otior*, and he only understands these three words and the respective perceptions that he associates with them, and he forgets what arose from their combination.

Another familiar example is *unus* (one) and *alterque* (the other); these are combined in the Latin word *uterque* (either). We should be very pleased if we had such a word in our modern languages as *uterque* to express such a concept. The French come closest to expressing it in the phrase *l'un et l'autre*; but they lack a single word that expresses the meaning,[*] and *uterque* gives a much clearer idea of it.

Let us take another instance in order to see the principle that I have in mind. You will of course all know the word *se*, the French word *se*, meaning 'self'. You know the word *hors* ('out' or 'outside', one could also say), and *tirer* (of which I shall retain only *tir*), meaning to pull, with-

---

[*] 'Either' conveys the meaning only in a very abstract way.—Translator.

draw. If you put these three elements together according to the same principle, you arrive at *sortir*, leave, go out, which is a combination of *se hors tir*, *tir* being the root of the verb *tirer*. So you can see this same all-prevailing intelligence in a modern language. Or take an example where the essential point is somewhat hidden through different linguistic layers: *coeur* (heart) and *rage* (a living, invigorating enthusiasm springing from the heart). When these two words are combined we get 'courage'. These are not arbitrary inventions but actual phenomena. It is in this way that words are formed.

But it is no longer possible today to form words in this way. Man has withdrawn from a living connection with the cosmic intelligence, and so at most only in very rare instances does he have an opportunity to venture into the domain of language in order to create words that could be said to be in the spirit of language. But the further back one goes, and especially the further one goes beyond the eighth century BC and explores the Greek and Latin languages, the more is the principle that brings about linguistic development active in a living context. And what is always so significant is that there is something of the nature of eurythmy in what one discovers in the case of a dead person, namely that he pulls words apart, he divides them into their parts. A dead person has more feeling for these parts of words than for entire words. If you think consistently through this whole process of development you would divide words into their sounds, and if you translate the sounds now not into stirrings of the breath but into movements of the whole human being you have eurythmy. So eurythmy is something that a dead person can well understand, if it is done to perfection. You can therefore see that things like eurythmy cannot be judged purely externally, and that one can understand its whole position in the overall context of human evolution only if one is also able to gain insight into this whole evolutionary process.

Much more could be said about the actual aim of eurythmy, but there will be an opportunity for this later on. I wanted initially to draw your attention to a sphere where, albeit in a shadowy way, human beings were in ancient times able to experience an interpenetration of the world of ideals into the everyday reality of their lives. I began by saying today that in our present world outlook we no longer find it possible to build a bridge between ideas, ideals and moral aspirations, on the one hand, and what lives in nature. The bridge is lacking. It is, moreover, perfectly natural that such a bridge is lacking in the present cycle of human evolution. The non-material world is no longer able to be creative. I wanted to show you an example in the human world itself (even though, as I have already said, it is somewhat indistinct) where a non-material influence is still working creatively within man. For in the combining of such words what was at work was not some kind of agreement between human beings or the deliberations of a single human individuality or personality but, rather, a higher intelligence and, moreover, without any real human contribution whatever. Today, of course, people want to be fully involved in everything they do; but you would soon see what would result from the level of wisdom that people have now if something so beautiful, great and meaningful as the formation of language were to be undertaken in our time! But it was precisely in those times when man was not as yet so inwardly involved that these awe-inspiring, wise and significant things occurred amongst mankind, and they happened in such a way that idea and reality worked together in close conjunction, in that a non-material, evolving intelligence and the actual movement of air interpenetrated the human organs of breathing. Today we are unable to build a bridge between the moral idea and something of the nature of electrical power; but here a bridge was built between something that was actually happening and something of an intelligent nature. As I shall elaborate tomorrow, this does not, of course, enable us to build the same bridge; it has to be built quite differently today. But you can see from this that mankind has advanced to its present state from another condition of existence, where he dwelt within a living, weaving activity which approximated to what takes place after death, albeit in a reverse direction. When a person dies in our time, he must—if he is to find his way forward between death and a new birth—separate out what has been joined together by forces (of which we shall speak tomorrow) in such a way that this process of union can still be clearly discerned if one goes back to the early stages of the forming of language.

These are important matters, matters that one really needs to consider if one seeks to address a question that we have often emphasized as being essential to keep in mind, namely how everything that is based on spiritual science should be incorporated into the whole fabric of contemporary intellectual and cultural life. If one speaks continually about the importance of enabling spiritual science to find its place in the whole evolutionary process, one needs also to think in a very practical way in this domain. In these lectures it is my intention to make a contribution to the practical, concrete thoughts that are needed. If it were possible for spiritual science to be brought into contemporary life by a certain movement, by a movement carried by human activity, spiritual science would be able to have a fructifying influence in every sphere. But there would naturally have to be the will to engage with such subtleties as have often been emphasized here. For we need to base what we may refer to as our own endeavour to place ourselves within the cultural movement of our time upon these subtleties, which always have a bearing upon the relationship of our spiritual science to the intellectual and cultural life of our present age. It is indeed the case that the tragic, catastrophic events of modern times should have made people aware that old world conceptions have now become completely bankrupt; and it will be through the relationship of spiritual science to these old world-conceptions rather than through what it can achieve in isolation that one will be able to see what needs to happen if we are to emerge from the bankruptcy of modern times.

In this connection it would indeed be necessary to focus upon the intentions that I have often spoken of as those of the spiritual-scientific movement. It would be really necessary to examine the reasons why it has, for example, on the one hand been so fruitful in some circles to work here on the building and why other endeavours of the Anthroposophical Society have in a certain sense remained equally unfruitful; why, if one disregards what it has indeed accomplished by placing the Dornach building in the world, it has nevertheless failed in so many ways. Such an achievement on the one side always means that much else is happening, when it does not—as frequently occurs—call forth the opposite. It would be essential that the Anthroposophical Society does not fail in other areas as well, as it has been completely failing over the years of its existence. There would be no need to keep on emphasizing this failure if it were far more widely recognized that it is important to try to understand why the Anthroposophical Society has failed in so many of its endeavours. If one were really to give the matter some thought one would, for example, come to understand on what basis the idea spreads that I would keep the Anthroposophical Society in leading-reins and make all the pronouncements; whereas there is scarcely a society in the world where less happens that a so-called leader would wish than in the Anthroposophical Society! By and large, what happens is the opposite of what I actually intend. So it is precisely in the Anthroposophical Society that one can see how in actual practical terms there is a wide gulf between reality and its so-called ideals. However, one must also have the will to stand firmly on the ground of reality. In a society there is, of course, a personal element; but one needs to recognize it as such. When people argue in some branch or other out of purely personal reasons, one should not turn white into black or black into white but, rather, simply admit that we have personal reasons, we like this person and not that one for reasons of this nature. This is being truthful; there is no need to turn reality into ideals. Thus it seems to be necessary that, whereas on the one hand I make every effort to lift everything of a spiritual-scientific nature out of the realm of sectarianism and eliminate everything of a sectarian nature, the Anthroposophical Society keeps falling into this rut ever more deeply and even enjoys being there. Whenever an effort is being made to escape from sectarianism, it is precisely this wish to escape from it that generates hate.

I do not of course want to blame anyone in particular or to be ungrateful for the fine efforts that are to be observed everywhere, and I fully appreciate everything; but there are many things that need to be considered if the kind of events that I have repeatedly heard about during these past days are not to occur again and again. These are, I may say, further instances of the personal element being entangled with the issue in question. When a disaster of some sort happens in a particular region, the way that the Anthroposophical Society is constituted is that when the Society feels like engaging in some minor bickering all these squabbles result in my being personally abused in the rudest fashion. When this keeps on happening again and again, we cannot make any progress. If I am being continually abused in this very rude way (because other people are squabbling and I am being manipulated as a result), it becomes impossible to sustain the presence of the anthroposophical movement in the world. It would be possible simply to work in a positive way if people were willing to adopt a more positive attitude, which I have been constantly advocating. It would be possible to put the sorts of things which for the most part rest on a very inferior foundation firmly behind one. But in many circles people have a far stronger inclination to indulge in quarrels and especially in dogmatic arguments, which often lead to personal disputes. And what then happens is that the abuse becomes focused on me. I am personally capable of keeping this at a distance, but the movement cannot continue to exist if things carry on in this way. In this particular case I am not reproaching anyone for what friends have done in a situation of this nature, but I need to point out that there is something else that they failed to do (and it is not for me to say blatantly what this is) which would have prevented what is continually happening far more surely than the way currently being attempted. The situation at present is that we only give [lecture] cycles to members of the Society,[16] and I realize that I am myself often considered odd by certain members of the Society if I am far more liberal as regards the distribution of cycles than members who are somewhat further removed would wish. Indeed, the harm done through outsiders exposing these cycles to the world can never match that which has been caused by members of the Anthroposophical Society! This must also be borne in mind. We have now reached the point where the cycles are being abused by members, by lapsed members of the Anthroposophical Society. So we are getting very close to saying that we shall no longer stipulate any boundaries, we shall sell the cycles to everyone who wants to have them. The situation could hardly be worse.

I am not saying that this is about to happen tomorrow, but I am merely indicating that the Society is functioning so completely not as it should be functioning (apart from the building and certain individual elements) that it is not doing those things that a society should be doing. The Society is therefore of no help whatsoever; it is not by any means what a movement should become.

It is very obvious that I am not referring to anyone personally and that I can say this completely without prejudice, for the simple reason that this is the very place where something fruitful is being done out of the Society, namely on the building. This is a real deed that has been accomplished by the Society. And if other things which could be much cheaper than the building were to work out of a similar social impulse to that found among those working on our building, immense blessings would flow from the Anthroposophical Society. But one would have to refer to both white and black by their true names. It is also important to note that where personal matters are concerned they really are personal affairs, and that they should not be hoisted up into a lofty idealism. One would have to consider what could take the place of the Anthroposophical Society. It could not be replaced by another society, because the same misery would simply be repeated! The Society cannot merely be a means whereby all sorts of inferior personalities keep wrangling with one another. However, it has become a place where one is forced constantly to pay attention to all manner of insignificant rubbish.

Well, I do not want to bore you any longer with all this, but I did want to add these remarks after finishing what I had to say. I had already brought the lecture to a close, and what I have now added is intended only as a brief initial statement.

LECTURE 8

TODAY I need to structure the studies that we are engaged in here in such a way that I shall enlarge upon what was presented yesterday, in order to arrive at some kind of provisional conclusion tomorrow. What is said today will therefore be more of the nature of an episode.

Events of the present time give one considerable reason to reflect about one thing or another, provided that one is not inclined to sleep through the most important impulses of our time. A particularly striking phenomenon which poses major questions at the present time and is one that must be familiar to you is the immeasurable untruthfulness that has taken hold today in the broadest sense, and specifically where a wider vision is being upheld. Phenomena such as the appearance of such a trenchant and radical untruthfulness are then also a stimulus for a spiritual-scientific investigation of everything associated with it. And in this respect one is frequently confronted by a fact that I have already mentioned on several occasions, namely that much of what is communicated to mankind as history is a kind of 'fable convenue'. The point here is not so much that facts that are communicated cannot be substantiated to a certain degree; what is more significant is that other facts—you may recall my telling you recently how the profound influence exercised by a certain person[1] has simply been deleted from Roman history—are obliterated. The Church has obliterated an immense amount of facts from history, because it was important to the Church that certain facts did not come to people's knowledge.

Yesterday we spoke from a certain point of view about the time which inaugurated the Graeco-Latin cultural epoch, namely the important period in the eighth century BC. It is a time of which historical traditions have little to impart. Although these traditions are full of uncertainty, one personality shines out from the beginning of this period of time who has succeeded in being studied in all sorts of different ways by a great number of people. From this early time shortly after the eighth century BC the name of Pythagoras lights up and also the name of the Pythagorean School. Yesterday I indicated that Pythagoras had been able to receive remnants of truths from the ancient Egyptian mysteries, and I gave something of the nature of these truths.

It is not only interesting to consider what Pythagoras and his pupils said and did, which was very far-reaching; for they did not only develop a school but were also very active politically. What Pythagoras and his pupils did is interesting, but it is important to study the world that surrounded their activities; for this was the world out of which Greek culture subsequently grew, influenced as it also was to a certain extent by the particular radiance that was embodied in Pythagoras. If one studies life in the seventh, sixth and fifth centuries BC, which was the prelude to the later Graeco-Roman age, if one studies life on the Greek peninsula, in the neighbouring countries and on the Italian peninsula, one is—provided that one is not looking in accordance with a preconceived picture but is being guided in one's studies by the light of truth for which spiritual-scientific research represents an essential contribution—struck by the prevalence of one particular human trait in this geographical context. There has hardly been a time when there has been so much lying as in the countries around the Mediterranean Sea in this period. Lying, telling people things that are untrue, was a very striking and characteristic quality of the life out of which Greek and Roman culture emerged.

One must not be under any illusions over such matters. All the immense beauty, the admirable wealth of imaginative creations of Greece and the most amazing number of abstract thoughts ever given to the world which were developed in Roman culture—all this grew, as does the plant world out of manure, from a foundation of human beings inhabiting the area around the Mediterranean who were completely impregnated with an obsessive passion for lying. This is something that is little spoken of in history, but it must be understood if one would gain any true insight into the declining period of the third post-Atlantean cultural period. As we approach the eighth century BC from the preceding centuries and millennia we are indeed passing through the declining period of this third post-Atlantean epoch of culture; and the people who were the bearers of the third post-Atlantean cultural period were consummate liars. This is also that epoch when the faculty of which I spoke to you yesterday and which is so extraordinarily interesting developed in a quite particular way, the faculty of forming language out of the cosmic power of reason. And alongside all these things that I explained to you yesterday, the greatest conceivable talent was invested at that time in the obsessive desire to lie.

If one is being properly realistic, one should no more allow oneself to be deluded about these things than about a violet which flowers in the spring and then fades and has within it these transient forces while it is in full bloom. In the violet the forces of coming into being and destruction follow one another in time. In human life, especially in the wider context of the life of humanity, these forces are very often engaged simultaneously, and we do not understand reality if we fail to see that things such as evolution (the potential for constructive activity, as for example in the forming of words and speech) and devolution (the devastating effect that lying has on one's inner life) take place alongside one another.

This is, as it were, the shadow side of what I spoke to you about yesterday. There is also a light side. This light side belongs more to the realm of spiritual-scientific research. Yesterday I already drew your attention to the fact that it would not be possible to speak with such certainty about the forming of language if the life of man after death did not provide clear proof of this process, in that words that are formed out of individual elements or portions of words here in life are again separated out into their different elements. This loosening process, this disintegration of words, is something that plays a significant part in the life of the dead. In a certain sense a dead person lives by virtue of this disintegration of words. Such a person has the very definite feeling that during his life—thus before his death—he was excluded from the spiritual world in which he now is through having formed composite words out of sounds and letters. A dead person has the feeling that language is like a curtain that is placed during his life between him and the spiritual world; and when the curtain is taken down and words are resolved into their constituent parts he has the feeling that he is again entering the spiritual world. Hence one of the characteristic actions of a dead person is to break up or pull to pieces the human words that the individual concerned learnt during his life between birth and death. He has, for example, a real sense of celebration when he manages to acquire a certain understanding as a result of this disintegration process. I have often spoken to you of how the moment of death is indeed from a certain point of view a fearful event as far as life in a physical body is concerned. People greatly prefer to avert their eyes from death. After death the spectacle of this event is, as I have often emphasized, always present, but there is nothing terrifying about it; for as a person contemplates his own death from the other side of existence he has in this spectacle the everlasting certainty that he is, and remains, an ego. I have often made this clear.

But the dead person now has to understand what is revealed to him from the other side of existence as he contemplates death. His understanding increases as he breaks up the words from whichever language he may have spoken. The ancient Hebrews and, somewhat similarly, also the Romans had their so-called holy names, the unutterable name of God, Jehovah or Yahweh. This unutterable name consisted for the Hebrews in a certain combination of the sounds experienced by us as the five vowels,[2] which were thought of as linked together during physical life. In the Roman Jovis (Jupiter) is concealed another form of the name Yahweh, where the five vowels are essentially being combined in a certain way. The dead person lived in the dissolution of what was combined in the name of God, and as he broke up the vowels that were brought together during life he had at the same time a revelation of what one might call the meaning of death. We must try to gain some sort of an inkling of what was revealed as the meaning of death. What we need to understand is that the meaning of death is revealed to the dead person through the dissolution of the holy name into its component parts, which then continue to sound forth throughout the universe. The dissolution of this holy name is associated with an understanding of the spiritualization of death. This is a concept that is extraordinarily difficult to describe. Death, when viewed from yonder side, can be referred to as a spiritualization. When we look at death from this point of view, what we perceive is associated with the arising of the spiritual dimension. Whereas one may experience this process of disintegration in a negative way as something ugly (as one does with anything destructive), this particular process of destruction, when viewed from yonder side of existence, manifests itself as a lighting up of the spiritual domain which, as it reverberates out into the universe, is then understood. It is as if the holy Word were sounding and raying forth, while disintegrating into the vowels of which it is composed, which then become audible as though from the periphery of the universe and enable the meaning of death, the spiritual meaning of death, to be understood as an aural experience.

This will lead you to see that it is justifiable to speak of the members of man's being that he possesses between death and a new birth, just as one speaks here in life of the physical body, ether body, astral body and ego. For now I have told you of the central experience that a person has between death and a new birth, namely the revelation of the spiritual meaning of death, the question must necessarily arise: what does this world that is revealed to human beings after their death look like? The only way to understand this is to come to know something about the nature and essential being of man himself.

Today we shall begin by trying to describe the person who has died as one would describe someone who is living. We can start with that member of the dead person that still has a considerable connection—not an affinity but a connection—with what man experiences between birth and death. The first member of human nature with which we are concerned is, therefore, what we can also call the 'I' or ego, which is what one calls the (initially) highest member of human nature between birth and death. Immediately after death it still initially retains the sheath of the ether body, which then dissolves in the course of time; these are aspects of it that do not actually belong to it. If one is speaking of the dead human being, the ego is the only member of this person who has died which can be recognized as being uniquely his own. I said that there is a connection with the ego of the earthly life, but there is no actual affinity; for in point of fact the ego manifests itself in a totally different way after death from how it is experienced between birth and death. Between birth and death the ego has a certain fluid quality, something that enables it to feel that it has the power to become different every day. Just imagine how dreadful it would be to live in a body between birth and death if you were not able to say to yourself: yesterday I did something I should not have done, but I can make amends, I can do something good to make up for it. Or suppose you were obliged to realize that you learnt very little in your earlier years but you are unable to learn anything more. At no moment in the life between birth and death is the ego so inflexible that it cannot bring about some sort of inner transformation through exerting its own will. What you experience as the ego after death is something that has become rigid, it has acquired certain qualities that cannot immediately be changed; it stays the way it is. The essential point to be grasped in order to understand the ego after death is the transformation of the constantly fluid nature of the ego between birth and death into a rigid structure where nothing is able to change, and which remains as it has become in the course of life. After death there is no question of a development such as we may attribute to the ego between birth and death. After death the ego is, as it were, a rigid spiritual structure that arises from a contemplation of death, and nothing about this ego can be changed. To put it plainly and simply, one might say that after death a person is condemned to see all the details of his life as something fixed. In the same way that, when you look out over a field, you see both the vegetation that is distant and close at hand all together and you do not see anything of a fluid nature but a fixed, extended and semi-permanent form, so do you behold the full extent of the course of your life not—as happens with life in a physical body—in a panorama where what is in the foreground merges into the background but as a definite and lasting vista where you are unable to change anything merely by looking at it. It would, moreover, fare badly with the dead person if this were not so; for the ego lays a considerable claim to what the gaze of a dead person beholds. He is as it were captivated by this ego. And were this ego to vanish from the scene, it would for the dead person be as if the world of the senses that surrounds the living were to disappear. It is indeed true to say that the

individual human being in his ego is actually as important to himself—
if I may put it thus—as the whole world of the senses that we share as
human beings is for the physical aspect of man's being. A vast abyss
would open up, an abyss of nothingness, if we were unable after death to
behold the ossified ego that has congealed out of its fluid state.

As a second member of man's being after death we have a kind of
spirit being that we can, by way of an analogy with what we already
know, also call the Spirit Self. The person concerned becomes conscious
of this spirit being mainly through this awareness of the Spirit Self rising
up as though from within. Whereas the ego offers a kind of outward
perspective, the consciousness of the Spirit Self emerges from within.
And to the same extent that one feels that this Spirit Self is inwardly
stirring, so does one become aware that the beings of the higher hierarchies are present. So if I am to avoid telling you something inaccurate
I would need to define it as I am writing it on the blackboard:[3] 'the
Spirit Self directed by the hierarchies towards the ego'.

What I have written accurately describes the situation. You have the
feeling that a being from the hierarchy of the Angeloi, or from the
hierarchy of the Exusiai, is now directing your gaze towards your ego.
By virtue of the fact that you are directing your gaze towards your ego,
at one time through the agency of a being of one hierarchy and at
another time because you know that your gaze is now being directed
towards your ego by a being of another hierarchy, you are getting to
know this hierarchy out of the activity of your Spirit Self. So you are
getting to know the hierarchies out of your own activity. You are
beginning to find yourself in the company of the hierarchies through
your Spirit Self. And whereas before this Spirit Self lights up you still
have the feeling that only you are engaged in directing your gaze
towards your own ego, you begin to feel ever more clearly that
increasing numbers of beings of the higher hierarchies are concerning
themselves with you and are becoming involved with your perception,
directing your gaze. As you develop your higher sense-activity you
increasingly feel through the Spirit Self that the beings of the higher
hierarchies are participating in this [supersensible] sense-activity. What
would be unendurable for people in the material world becomes the
very element of life in the condition that they inhabit after death.

Just imagine that you were standing here at the window and looking out at the surroundings. The person sitting nearest comes up and turns your head in order to enable you to see something in that direction. Then a second person comes and inclines your head slightly upwards so that you see something else again; and so the whole company of people sitting here approach you from behind, and the aspect of your outward surroundings that you see would depend on the people sitting here continually turning your head this way or that. If you now think of this not as viewed from outside but as an inner experience, an inner feeling, you have a true analogy of this experience that you have as your Spirit Self. You increasingly make yourself part of the life of the higher hierarchies through these higher hierarchies entering into the directing of your gaze.

The beings of the higher hierarchies are also involved in the dissolution of words of which we have already spoken. This is one aspect of what is experienced then. But this ever-increasing familiarity with the hierarchies leads to a continual enrichment of life. Moreover, in a wholly similar way one gets to know the beings with whom one had some kind of karmic connection before death. One feels that one is being led or guided. This is what can be said about the second member of man's being in the life between death and a new birth.

What can be said about the third member may perhaps come as something of a shock to one's ordinary human understanding. As one participates in this life after death one gradually feels that one is being imbued with a certain power, with what I might perhaps describe as a nexus of forces. After one has initially felt the hierarchies approaching and guiding one in a supersensible sense-activity (if I may express it in this way), one gradually feels that these hierarchies are gently imbuing one with power, with a certain force. One has the feeling of being gradually filled with this power that the hierarchies bring with them as they enter into us, as they delicately engage their essential being with us. One gradually becomes sensitive to this power. One feels not only that one's attention is directed by the hierarchies towards this or that but that one is oneself inwardly filled with strength as a result of this activity of the hierarchies, which manifests itself as an activity that facilitates visionary perception. We feel the forces of the cosmos itself streaming into us like enlivening fluids. But what is so startling is that the forces that we now feel streaming into us are of a quite particular kind. They are forces that quite definitely do not promote life as we know it in the physical world; rather do they disintegrate and destroy it. We feel ourselves gradually being filled with a cosmic, death-bringing power.

It is important to be open to such extraordinary ideas, because only in this way can the spiritual world be properly understood. Just imagine your soul and spiritual nature being gradually filled with forces of which, as you inwardly experience them, you have the awareness that everything that lives here on the Earth would be killed if you were to come in contact with it. So in the third place you clothe yourself in what by way of an analogy with something we already know we can call the Life Spirit. You clothe yourself in something that one can call the Life Spirit, but its most distinctive quality is that it is fatal to the functioning of the life body. You therefore acquire a third member of your being which enables you to kill every ether body that comes across your path. Everything that you contact through this member of your being becomes dead in the sense that one speaks of death here on Earth. And as you kill by means of these forces that you receive, you awaken spiritual life—or, initially, actually soul life—from what has been killed. It is indeed an extraordinary experience to encompass that the living is killed through contact with the living, but soul life is brought into being, is released, by this killing. It is a death-bringing process, but it is at the same time a liberation of soul forces from the fetters of life. Thus one can say that the Life Spirit kills the earthly aspect of the living, releasing within it forces of soul. And the source of this remarkable experience is that soul forces are in a sense enchanted within what is living, and that through the process which is enacted after death the enchanted soul forces are liberated from out of the living. One might be inclined to see something terrible and repellent in the destructive way in which the force of which we have been speaking works. This is not by any means the case in so far as the life after death is concerned, because in this death-bringing power there resides a continual illumining of soul life, a capacity to kindle soul life into being. Moreover, the dead person needs to have this consciousness: not only so that he can contemplate the death that he has himself undergone but he also has to be conscious of the fact that the essential nature of his death is spread over the whole foundation of what he now experiences in the spiritual world. It is as if one henceforth lives in the spiritual world in such a way that one can say that here in the spiritual world forms of a spiritual nature are continually arising—although initially they are actually forms of soul life; and soul life is engendered in a variety of different ways. But if one were to ask about the nature of the soil whence all this soul substance springs forth, the source is the death-bringing force of which we have just been speaking. And so a power that destroys ordinary life on Earth becomes the essential soul nature that we need to acquire between death and a new birth, just as in earthly life we have to acquire our carnal body.

A fourth member of man's being between death and a new birth may—again, by analogy with what we already know—be called the Spirit Man. Spirit Man in this connection is experienced in such a way that, in addition to the forces with which one has already been imbued by the hierarchies (as I have already described), one is impregnated with the possibility not only of killing and destroying life—that is, what we call life here on Earth—and bringing it to a state of disintegration but of utterly destroying forms and translating them into different forms. {The following words were written on the blackboard.}

1. The ego
2. The Spirit Self   directed *by* the hierarchies towards the ego
3. The Life Spirit   kills what is known in the earthly sense as the living, releasing within it forces of soul
4. The Spirit Man

It does, of course, become more and more difficult to describe these things. But essentially the force of the Spirit Man as it lives in a human being between death and a new birth is such that one thereby carries out an activity that is the very opposite of what can be associated in the widest sense with the engendering of forms. To take a specific example, here on Earth one draws triangles, squares and so forth. After death, by virtue of the forces that are being developed in this realm, one does the opposite: one dissolves all the forms that one has drawn. But the strange thing is that this does not simply mean that a form is done away with; it is at the same time a cosmic activity. One is oneself in the midst of cosmic activity, connected with cosmic activity; for this deconstruction process, this dissolving of forms, is a cosmic activity, and when a [dead] person who has been imbued with the Life Spirit acquires this power of deconstruction, this power of dissolving forms, he has become part of the cosmic world. He works within the cosmos itself.

What has to do with destruction and decline here on Earth is closely associated with the processes of coming into being and formation in the spiritual worlds, and vice versa; what appears here as destruction and decline, deconstruction and dissolution of form, has a lot to do with coming into being in yonder worlds of spirit. So when I speak of deconstruction and dissolution of form I am not speaking of decline in the spiritual world but only of decline in the world of soul—and I am indeed speaking of the appearance of something spiritually new in the spiritual world.

Many mysteries in the world have a connection with these things. As you approach the southern part of Italy from the central part of the country today you will find regions that are poor and not particularly fertile, where only a meagre amount of nature's riches are available to human beings. These are the same regions where Pythagoras was active at the dawn of the fourth post-Atlantean epoch—and in his day Pythagoras was working in an area that was very fertile, abundant and luxuriant. It has been such a short time since that period; and yet if we consider this little portion of the Earth where Pythagoras was active we can see the transformation from a fertility and luxuriance that was on a Sybaritic[4] scale to poverty, even to the point where serious illnesses arise. Instead of a budding, luxuriant life such as existed in those times where historical research has little access, something has developed which in comparison to that luxuriant, vigorous life amounts to a real poverty of nature. It is highly interesting to observe such transitions in the outer world, where coming into being and passing away are perpetually interlinked. However, those engaged in historical research are not so advanced in their thinking that they make the right connections between those continual processes of coming into being and passing away. Pythagoras developed his activities amidst vigorous luxuriance where lying was rife, and the influence of these activities continued after his death; and what Pythagoras and the Pythagorean souls had to accomplish after their death is connected in many ways with what came to be manifested in the decline of the blossoming, sprouting life in the midst of which Pythagoras lived. Pythagoras and the souls of his followers were not wholly without a share in the work of destruction— which for yonder world is a task of bringing something into being— that arose in the period after Pythagoras in the place where nature was formerly luxuriant and plentiful. In order to understand the world as a whole, one has to get used to the idea that things look quite different depending on whether one's viewpoint is here between birth and death or between death and a new birth. Someone who would be committing a crime if he were arbitrarily to destroy a rich and abundant life in the earthly domain is merely doing something that happens as an eternal necessity when he participates in an endeavour between death and a new birth that here on Earth clearly signifies decline and decay.

Something was meant to come to an end with the third post-Atlantean epoch, and this left its shadows behind it. Much had to come to an end in a different domain from the one that has just been referred to. This declining aspect of the third post-Atlantean epoch has a significant bearing on the prevalence of lying at that time. The reason for all this lying on the Earth was that people were, as I explained yesterday, still connected with cosmic forces; but the cosmic forces that exerted their influence upon earthly evolution before the eighth century BC were in many ways of a deceitful nature. Demonic liars were active in the sphere into which the soul of man entered while he was developing words, as I described this process yesterday. He had, so to speak, to extend the head region of his soul into a sphere where he could do this: the sphere of cosmic reason or intelligence. But within this sphere there were those ahrimanic forces that came to expression in the activity of countless lying demons. And out of this same source whence the language-forming power of that time was derived there developed this colossal power of lying on the soil of Mediterranean culture. People lied because the demons who introduced the capacity of forming languages were liars. It was the task of these demonic liars to bring about the decline of what had to decline in order that the third post-Atlantean period could come to an end and the fourth one could take its place.

The world is ordered in accordance with necessities, and one needs to pay attention to these necessities if one is seeking to answer the great question that we posed at the beginning of our studies yesterday—the question of the connection of the moral and the non-material realm of ideas with the processes of nature. I shall speak further about this tomorrow, thereby bringing these studies to a provisional conclusion.

Lecture 9

DORNACH, 2 SEPTEMBER 1918

THE studies in which we have been currently engaged concern matters that many of those people who know something about them in one form or another regard as mysteries. There are specific reasons why knowledge of these things is withheld from the world on a very broad scale, since the opinion is held that those particular things that are being considered are aspects of an extensive knowledge of supersensible affairs that should not yet be imparted to humanity today. I consider this view in so far as it pertains to certain matters that are being spoken about here to be mistaken, on the grounds that it appears to me to be necessary for mankind to make the courageous resolve to engage in a real study of the supersensible worlds. And the only way of achieving this is that one directly takes hold of what addresses the question under consideration in a specific way.

Today I should first of all like to deal with a sort of preliminary question. We spoke yesterday about the members of man's being between death and a new birth. A very widespread objection to the discussing of these matters—not on the part of initiates but from the uninitiated—is that one simply says: well now, why is it necessary to know anything about such things? It would be better to wait until one has passed through the gate of death, and one will see perfectly well what it is really like in the spiritual world. This is something that is often said. Now the fact of the matter is that we can never answer such questions from a hard and fast standpoint where we are speaking of realities, for in a spiritual-scientific context we always have to respond to them from the standpoint of the times in which we are living. We live in the fifth post-Atlantean epoch, which began in the fifteenth century AD. It was then, as we know, that the fourth post-Atlantean epoch, which began in the eighth century BC, came to an end. Seven such cultural epochs may be distinguished. One can discern from this that we have passed beyond the middle of the cultural development of the Earth, which had its focal point in the fourth post-Atlantean epoch, and that by virtue of this fact—and we are, moreover, in the fifth great period of the Earth—we have entered the time in which the Earth is in a descending phase of evolution.

The studies in which we have been engaged in the course of these days may make you aware that we are dealing with a descending phase of evolution, with a process which is not so much one of evolution as of devolution, an evolution that has a retrogressive aspect. Our entire earthly evolution is in a retrogressive phase. Certain faculties and forces which were present in the previous period of an ascending evolution have now ceased their activity, and others now have to take their place. This is especially the case with regard to certain of man's inner faculties of soul. One can say that until the fourth post-Atlantean epoch and roughly until the time of the Mystery of Golgotha human beings still had the faculties that enabled them to have a certain connection with the supersensible world. As we know, these faculties have disappeared in all manner of different ways. They are no longer present as elemental capacities—they have simply ceased to exist. Not only has man's life on Earth between birth and death changed with respect to such faculties but there has even—and more radically—been a change in his life between death and a new birth. With respect to this period between death and a new birth it has to be said that in the present cycle of human evolution, which is already in a descending phase, human beings will on passing through the gate of death need to have specific memories of what they have acquired here in the physical body, if they are to find a right attitude and a right relationship to the events to which they are exposed between death and a new birth. Indeed, one of the necessary prerequisites for a life after death that is as it should be is that human individuals should before death increasingly acquire certain conceptions about the life after death; for only if they remember these ideas which they have acquired here on Earth will they be able to orientate themselves in the time between death and a new birth. It is objectively untrue to assert that it would be possible to wait until death to concern oneself with such notions about life between death and a new birth. If people continue to cling to these prejudices, if they firmly refuse to try to explore such ideas about life between death and a new birth, this life—this disembodied existence—would become dark and disorientating for them; in the absence of everything that I described to you yesterday, they would be unable to enter in the right way into their spiritual surroundings. Until close to the time of the Mystery of Golgotha it was the case that people brought faculties into physical life which derived from the spiritual world; and this was the source of their atavistic clairvoyance. As you are well aware, the existence of this atavistic clairvoyance arose from the fact that certain spiritual faculties radiated into this life from the pre-natal condition. But instead of this the reverse now needs to happen: human beings increasingly need to acquire here on the Earth some conception of life in the post-mortem state, life after death, in order that they may be able to carry something of what they remember of this through the gate of death.

This is what I particularly want to say concerning this preliminary question. Thus the flippant talk of being able to wait until death before acquiring such thoughts is of no account if one clearly bears in mind the period of earthly evolution in which we are living. One must always keep an eye on specific details. For standpoints that are valid in the absolute sense, that are valid for all time, do not exist; there are only perceptions which can give man orientation for a certain period of time. This is a spiritual-scientific truth that one simply has to assimilate.

And now I should like to embark upon something that can bring our studies to a provisional conclusion. We started out by saying that people today are aware of a gulf between what they refer to as ideals, whether of a moral kind or from other source, and ideas, on the one hand, and what they perceive to be their views about the natural world order. The concepts and views that people have about the natural world order do not permit them to accept that the ideals that they bear within their hearts have any real power or can become realities as is possible for forces of nature.

The important point to be considered here is as follows. We now have an awareness of the way that man's being is ordered here on the physical Earth. We also have some knowledge of the organization of man's being in the spiritual world between death and a new birth. Some while ago I posed a question which confronts anyone who takes life seriously in a very real way but is the precise kind of question that one cannot even remotely address if one is aware of the aforesaid gulf between idealism and realism. The question is: why is it that in our world order many people die young, either already as children or as young people or in the prime of life, whereas others die when they are old? What connection does this have with the ordering of the world? Neither idealism, on the one hand, nor realism, which is unable to regard ideals as real forces, on the other can properly address such questions, which are nonetheless vital questions. One can, in fact, approach such questions only if one takes something quite specific into consideration. One needs to bear in mind that man as he is constituted today as an earthly human being relates fairly readily to space but not with equal facility to time. Modern philosophical viewpoints as a whole do not offer any conclusion that is worth mentioning, and the question of the essential nature of time has hitherto been addressed only amongst very limited circles of people. It is, moreover, not so easy to speak in a layman's language about time and its essential nature, but it may perhaps be possible to give you an idea of what I actually mean if I speak of time by making an analogy with space. I will have to make a claim on your patience, because the brief elucidation that I want to make appears to have a somewhat abstract character (although it really is only apparently so).

If you simply view a portion of the world of space you know that what you can see manifests itself to you in accordance with the laws of perspective. You have to take perspective into account if you are viewing a portion of the spatial world. If you now transpose the portion of the spatial world that you are looking at, and to which you instinctively ascribe the quality of perspective, to a flat surface, you take perspective into account. Thus when, for instance, you look down an avenue, you see its more distant trees smaller and closer together. You can express this in perspective by bringing what you see in space to expression on a surface in this sort of way

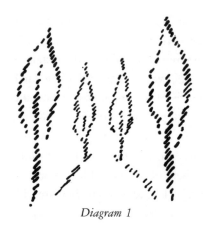

Diagram 1

It is obviously the case that what you see in space is adjacent on a flat surface. In space the objects are not next to one another; here you have two trees in the foreground, while two others are in the far distance [see Diagram 1]. But by bringing the portion of space that is being observed onto a surface, you place objects that are actually behind one another side by side. By contrast, you have the instinctive capacity to translate what you see painted or drawn on a surface into a spatial dimension. The reason why you have this capacity is that man as he is now as an earthly human being has to a considerable extent liberated himself from space as such.

Man has not freed himself from time in the same way. This is a fact of immense and far-reaching importance, but it is unfortunately hardly noticed—at any rate by science. Because they evolve in time, people think that they have an overview of time, that they know all about time; but as a matter of fact they do not know about real time. What they experience as time is not real time at all; its relationship to real time is something that one might call a reflection. What they generally refer to as time is related to real time in the same way that this picture [see drawing] on a flat surface is related to space. Generally speaking, people do not experience real time; rather do they experience a reflection of time, a mere image of its real nature. This can be very difficult to imagine.

It is, for example, extraordinarily difficult to envisage that something that is exerting an influence today does not need to belong to the present but has its real existence in a much earlier period of time and is not a reality in the present. You can see what was present in a very early period working as though in perspective into your own time.

What I have just said has a very significant consequence, namely that everything that we call nature has an altogether different character from all that we must regard as being a certain part of man himself. Ahriman, for example, is active in nature—and one can say the same of ahrimanic forces. But ahrimanic forces are never an active force in nature in a present context. If you look at nature as a whole, Ahriman is indeed to be found working there; but his activity derives from a far distant time. Ahriman works from the past. And whether you are surveying the mineral, the plant or the animal kingdom you should never be saying that Ahriman is active in anything that is spread out before your eyes at the present time. Nevertheless, Ahriman is active in all of this—but from the past. So if I were to present what I am saying in the form of a diagram, I would have to say: here is the line of evolution from the past to the future, and here you are surveying the natural world.

Past

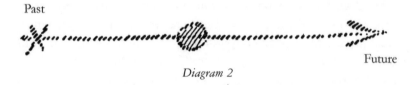

Future

Diagram 2

Yes, you must imagine that you are looking at the world of nature from this point. There is no trace of ahrimanic forces in what you are surveying as a present reality, but the influence of Ahriman is exerted upon nature from the past, from a specific period in the past.

When, moreover, you become aware of Ahriman in nature, he appears to you in a kind of temporal perspective. If you were to say that Ahriman is active in the present, you would be making the same mis-

Past

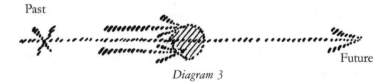

Future

Diagram 3

take with regard to nature as if you were to say: When I look at a scene in space, the trees in the far distance are beside those in the foreground (on the grounds that they can be placed in perspective on a flat surface). [See Diagram 1.]

A fundamental requirement for a true perception of the spiritual world is that one learns to see in perspective in a temporal sense, that one learns to place every being in the point of time where it belongs.

When I told you yesterday that the ego after death is in a certain sense transmuted from a condition of mobility into one that is more fixed, that is not all that is to be said on this subject and something more needs to be added. Let us suppose that you had been living here on Earth with your ego from 1850 until 1920, and in 1920 you became aware of your ego. What I mean is this: you will probably have been aware of it before, but now you look back, you look back upon your ego with the Spirit Self through the hierarchies, and you see that your ego has been at a constant standstill from 1850 until 1920. The ego is present, but it does not progress. This means that your experiences do not accompany you shortly after your death but instead you look back at them, you look back on them from a perspective that is distant in a temporal sense; and you perceive a sequence of time just as you perceive spatial distance here in the physical world. I can also express it as follows. If, shall we say, you die in 1920, you go on living with all that I have described to you yesterday as the members of your being; but you look back at the stretch of time when you have been living here on Earth with your ego. This stretch of time remains as it is, and you continue to see it where it belongs in the time sequence, inasmuch as you are living with a sense of perspective. It is in such a way that you must picture Ahriman involved in external nature, though from a former point in time.

This is very important, and it is something that is barely considered. If one is wanting to understand the world, if one wants to speak about time in a spiritual-scientific way, one must conceive of time in a spatial-like way and take this on-going connection of reality with time into account. This is very important.

Now what I have said with regard to the ahrimanic powers, namely that they work from out of the past, is correct as far as nature is con-

cerned. But the situation with man is different. In the course of man's
life between birth and death, everything that takes place in time
becomes maya or illusion for him. While he lives here on Earth he
himself lives in the course of time, and by living a certain number of
years he lives through this temporal sequence along with them. As time
passes, so does he himself accompany it. This is not the case with space.
If you walk down an avenue, the trees remain behind as you move
forwards, and you do not take the trees that have remained behind—
thus also your impressions of them—along with you in such a way that
as you take a step you had the idea that your image of the trees is
accompanying you. This is what you do in the case of a temporal image.
Because you are yourself evolving in time, what you actually do in the
physical body is that over time you surrender to an illusion with regard
to your perspective. You do not notice the perspective of time, and the
subconscious part of our human nature is particularly unaware of it.
Man's subconsciousness is really blind to this aspect of living with time
and has a totally illusory relationship to the perspective of time. This
does, however, have a quite specific consequence, which is that ahrimanic forces are enabled to work within man as forces belonging to the
present. Ahrimanic forces exert an influence upon man's inner life as
forces of the present. So this is how man relates to nature. As he looks
out upon nature, there is nothing ahrimanic in the present, but it works
in fact as maya, as an illusion. But man has surrendered himself to this
illusion with regard to what I have been explaining to you, with the
result that the ahrimanic powers gain through man the possibility of
creeping into the present, of migrating into our present time. We can
say that the ahrimanic powers—and the same also applies to the luciferic powers, although from a somewhat different aspect of which we
shall speak shortly—are active in nature in such a way that they do not
actually have anything to do with the present but are extending their
influence into it from an earlier period of time; whereas within man
these ahrimanic powers are working as a present reality.

What is the consequence? The consequence of this is that, because of
the point that I have just been making, man is unable to feel any
relationship to nature in his deepest inner being. He observes his own
being and is aware of his feelings, while sensing the working of nature's

laws. Because ahrimanic forces are present-day realities within him whereas in nature they are forces from the past, everything that is in accordance with nature appears to him to be different from what is evolving within his own being. He does not understand the difference that he observes between himself and nature in the right way. Were he to resolve it in the right way it would be as I have just explained. He would say: Out there in nature Ahriman's influence extends from out of the past; in me Ahriman is active as a force belonging to the present. What happens as a result is that, while he may not be conscious of the difference, he acts in accordance with it; and he experiences nature as devoid of spirit. He may no doubt feel that the ahrimanic forces are not working directly within nature at the present time, but he experiences nature as devoid of spirit because, rather than say to himself that Ahriman is working from out of the past, he sees nature only as it is now; and Ahriman is no longer active there.

Now however strange it may sound, Ahriman is nonetheless that power which is used by the creative powers of the world to bring nature into being. When one speaks of the spirit of nature, of the true spirit of nature, one should actually be speaking of the spirit of Ahriman. Here Ahriman is fully justified. The beings of the normal hierarchies make use of the ahrimanic spirit to bring about the nature that is spread every-where around us. The reason why we do not experience nature as permeated with spirit is that the spirit is not included in the present life of nature but its influence extends from out of the past. This, I may say, is the secret of the creative powers of the world, that they make use of a spirit whom they have allowed to remain at an earlier stage to exert his influence at a later stage, while enabling him to work from out of the past.

When we are speaking of nature, we should be speaking neither of matter nor of forces but, rather, of ahrimanic beings; but we should be speaking in such a way that we place these ahrimanic beings in the past. Thus a strange thing emerges from this. Imagine some philosopher of nature who is speculating about what lies behind all the phenomena of nature. Well, he forms all kinds of theories and hypotheses about atomic relationships and the like. But this is not the point. Behind what is spread out around us and visible to our senses is not what the philosophers of nature generally suppose to be there, because behind all this is the totality of ahrimanic forces, though not as present realities. If, therefore, the philosopher of nature feels obliged to postulate the existence of atomic structures of some sort behind the chemical elements, he would be mistaken; behind the chemical elements are ahrimanic forces. Were you to be able to unveil and look behind what you see of the chemical elements, you would not see anything there at present. Where people look for atoms it would be hollow, and what is active there is working into this hollow space from out of the past. This is how it is in reality. Hence these numerous unfortunate theories regarding what the 'thing in itself' is; for this 'thing in itself' is not there at all at present. In the place where people look for the 'thing in itself', there is nothing; but the influence there derives from the past. So one could say that when Kant[1] was searching for his 'thing in itself', he should have said: I cannot approach what I am wanting to reach as the 'thing in itself'. This is what he did also say. But he did not realize that he had not found anything at all belonging to the present, and that if he had gone behind the veil of phenomena and had gone far back into the past he would have found the ahrimanic powers.

With man himself the situation is different. Through the very fact that man participates in time as a living being, it has been possible for the ahrimanic powers to gain entry to our world through the portal of humanity and to work in a corresponding way within man. The consequence of this activity of the ahrimanic powers in man is that he disconnects what he sees in the present from the spirit, that he separates his present existence from the spiritual domain. This is the result of the fact that we bear ahrimanic forces in the state of maya within us. Thus one can say that our perception of the world as a material entity bereft of spirit, as a mere natural order whose culmination is thought to be found in the law of the conservation of energy and matter (which is an illusion), that this is what we regard to be the natural order is entirely due to the circumstance that we bear ahrimanic forces within us and not that they exist in nature as forces of the present. Our conception of nature as something conceived of in a purely material way does not, therefore, correspond with nature as such but only with nature as it is at present. But this present reality of nature is an abstraction, because Ahriman's influence upon it is always exerted from out of the past.

However, not only is an ahrimanic influence active within man but also one emanating from Lucifer. This luciferic influence has in a certain sense a different tendency in the universe from that of Ahriman, which we can visualize in the way that we have been describing. Ahriman's influence within us tends towards a materialistic conception of the world. That we conceive of the world in a materialistic way and think only in terms of a natural order is the result of the ahrimanic influence that we bear within us; whereas our propensity to cherish ideals that are disconnected from the world of nature, ideals in accordance with which we would wish to govern our mutual relationships but which in the context of our present world-conception necessarily have the quality of mere dreams that will vanish into oblivion when the Earth has reached the end-point determined for it by natural law, is the consequence of the constant striving of the luciferic forces, which live in us as do the ahrimanic forces, to wrench that part of us that is accessible to them wholly out of the natural order and to spiritualize it in its entirety. The main tendency of the luciferic forces, in so far as they dwell within us, is to make us as spiritual as possible, to tear us wherever possible away from material life of any kind. They therefore lead us to believe in ideals that have no validity in the natural world and are powerless in the present world order. If in the course of future earthly periods man were wholly to succumb to the luciferic influence, so that he believed that ideals are mere intellectual formulations to which feelings must be subordinate, he would be following the powers of Lucifer. The material Earth to which we belong would disintegrate, would disappear without trace in the cosmic expanses and would fail to fulfil its purpose, and the luciferic powers would lead man to another spiritual world to which he does not belong. To this end they need to employ the stratagem of leading us to believe in ideals that are actually mere dreams. Just as Ahriman, on the one hand, deceives us with a world that is nothing but a natural order, so does Lucifer, on the other hand, present us with a world that consists only of fabricated ideals.

This is something that is highly significant; and at present some kind of adjustment can only be made in those regions that lie in the unconscious areas of man's being. Human beings, must, however, become increasingly conscious of these matters, otherwise they will not extricate themselves from this dilemma or succeed in building the necessary bridge between idealism and realism.

What creates some kind of adjustment in our time is the following. When at present young people die, for example children, these children (and it is similar with all young people) have only glimpsed at the world; they have not fully lived out their lives on the physical plane. They arrive in the other world—the world between death and a new birth, which unfolds in the way I described yesterday—with a life that has not been fulfilled on the physical plane. By living only a part of their earthly life, they bring something into the spiritual world from the earthly life that one cannot bring when one has become old. One enters the spiritual world differently when one has grown old from if one dies young. If one dies young, one has lived one's life in such a way that one still has many of the forces that one had before birth in the spiritual world. Because of this one has established an intimate connection between the spiritual forces that one has brought with one and the physical existence that one has experienced here; and through this intimate connection it is possible to take into the spiritual world something of what has been acquired on the Earth. Children and others who have died young take into the spiritual world something from the earthly life that cannot by any means be carried over by someone who dies as an older person. What is carried over in this way is then in the spiritual world; and what children and young people bring with them gives the spiritual world a certain gravity which it would not otherwise have, thus giving this same spiritual world in which people are living together a quality that prevents the luciferic powers from completely severing the connection between the spiritual and physical worlds.

Just think what a tremendous mystery we are beholding here! When children and young people die, they take something with them from here by means of which they impede the luciferic powers in their efforts to separate us completely from earthly life. It is of the greatest importance that one keeps this in mind.

If one lives longer here on the Earth, one cannot upset the calculations of the luciferic powers in the same way; for from a certain age one no longer has that intimate connection between what one brought with one at birth and physical earthly life. Once a person has become old this inner connection is dissolved, and the exact opposite now occurs. From a certain age onwards we gradually imbue the spiritual aspect of the physical Earth with our own being. We make the physical Earth more spiritual than it would have been otherwise. Thus from a certain age we spiritualize the physical Earth in a certain way that is imperceptible to the senses. We bring a spiritual quality to the physical Earth, just as we endow the spiritual world with a physical quality when we die young; when we grow old we exude a certain spirituality—I cannot express it in any other way. From a spiritual point of view growing old consists in a sense of exuding a spiritual quality here on the Earth. In this way the calculations of Ahriman are upset. It is because of this that Ahriman cannot in the long run have so intense an influence on human beings today that their conviction that ideals have a certain significance can be completely extinguished. Nevertheless, we are at present very close to a situation where people will fall prey to the most dreadful errors with regard to these very things. Even well-meaning people will easily succumb to such errors in this particular area. These errors will grow to an ever greater magnitude, and as earthly evolution advances they may well assume gigantic proportions.

To give you an example, there is a really intelligent philosopher called Robert Zimmermann[2] who in 1882 wrote a book called *Anthroposophy*. I have already mentioned this in a certain context. This 'anthroposophy' is not what we now call anthroposophy, it is more or less a tangle of different concepts; but this is because Robert Zimmermann could not see into the spiritual world and was merely a Herbartian philosopher. Nevertheless, he has written this *Anthroposophy*. But in this *Anthroposophy* Robert Zimmermann concerns himself from his own standpoint with the question that in the course of these days I have placed on the top of our agenda. On the one hand he sees ideas, logical ideas, aesthetic ideas, ethical ideas; on the other he sees the natural order. And he is completely unable to find a bridge from these logical, aesthetic and ethical ideas to the natural order but instead holds firmly to the thought that on the one hand there is the natural world and on the other the world of ideas. His conclusion is, in fact, extraordinarily interesting, for it is thoroughly typical of someone today. He ends up by saying that it is inherently impossible for man to furnish nature with ideas and to endow ideas with a force of nature. The two worlds can actually only be brought together in people's heads. This is what he says. Hence in one context where he is summing up everything that he is saying and thinking he makes the following statement: 'The realization of ideas belongs neither to the past nor to the present but is a task whose fulfilment lies in the future and in the hands of human beings. The dream of a "golden age" regarding which a sober rationalist like Kant (in the form of his notion of "everlasting peace") and an extreme positivist like Comte[3] (in his *état positif*) went into such raptures, will be fulfilled when the whole world of ideas becomes real and the whole of reality is imbued with ideas. That is to say, when what Schiller[4] called "the secret art of the master", the "extermination of matter through form" is made manifest or, in the words of Schleiermacher,[5] "when ethics have become physics and physics ethics".'

Yes—but this can never be! The only way that this can happen is for human beings to bring ideas to fulfilment in their social organization. But when the Earth has come to an end the whole dream-world of ideas will have vanished. No other outcome is possible according to such a philosophy. Hence a philosophy of this nature always remains abstract and must ultimately arrive at the following position:[6] 'A philosophy such as this is not, like theosophy, based on a theosophical standpoint *inaccessible to* human knowledge and which considers the "dream of reason" to be something long since realized, nor does it, like anthropology, rest upon the admittedly anthropocentric but nevertheless *uncritical* standpoint of common experience, which regards a reality penetrated with ideas as a mere "dream of reason"; it is at once *anthropocentric*, that is, it emanates from human experience, and yet also *philosophy*, because it seeks to reach out beyond experience by way of logical thought. I therefore call it *anthroposophy*.' So 'anthroposophy' is here the admission that one can never bridge the gulf between unreal ideas and a reality bereft of ideas.

Now there is in man himself a being of nature which therefore belongs to the natural order, while having a connection with a spiritual being who can receive spiritual substance. An anthroposophist such as

Robert Zimmermann does not deny this. But the way that man is regarded by modern science is such that the riddle cannot be solved by man, by the microcosm.

Let us now recall something that we have already mentioned during these days. We said that we must actually divide man into three parts—not, of course, so simply as with the skeleton, as I have already explained. However, I have also spoken about this in the concluding notes of my book *The Riddles of the Soul*.[7] We can divide man into three parts: the head, the trunk and the extremities; the latter term encompasses everything that relates internally to the extremities, including the sexual organs. If we divide man's being in such a way and now turn to something that we already know—that the form or shape of the head is indicative of forces from the previous incarnation and actually only the middle region of the trunk belongs to the present—then after what I have explained today you will no longer find it so incredible if I tell you this about the head. The head that a person bears goes back to the previous incarnation, to the past. Forces from the past, ahrimanic forces, exert their influence upon the head, and what applies to ahrimanic forces in general is of particular validity for the human head. Everything relating to the form of the human head does not really belong to the present, for the head is a receptive vessel for the forces of the previous incarnation; and the creative powers make use of the ahrimanic powers in order to form our head, in order to give our head the form that it has. If the creative powers were not to avail themselves of the ahrimanic spirits to form our head, we would—forgive me, but this is how it is—in addition to having a much softer head all have the head of an animal: one person who is like a bull in his character would have a bull's head, another person who has the nature of a lamb would have a lamb's head, and so on. It is due to the influence of the ahrimanic forces that are made use of by the creative powers to give us our form that this animal head which we would otherwise have to bear does not actually crown our bodies, as the Egyptians depicted many of their figures; that we are spared from going about looking like these Egyptian figures (which had good reason to look as they did, because such things were also taught in the Egyptian mysteries, albeit from an atavistic standpoint, and are sometimes also taught today); and that, moreover, we do not go around as they did in Rosicrucian pictures,[8] where every woman is painted with a lion's head and every man with that of an ox. This was how the Rosicrucians painted human beings. They chose a more average kind of animal and therefore gave women a lion's head, which for the most part had a greater resemblance to women, while the men were given the head of an ox or bull, because of its greater resemblance to them. So when you see Rosicrucian figures of a man and a woman placed next to one another, the woman with her beautiful leonine head and the man with that of a bull, this is perfectly correct. That the metamorphosis—I mean this now in a Goethean sense—is able to take its course, that our head which in its form has a tendency towards the animal nature is formed in accordance with its human shape, we owe to the influence of the ahrimanic powers. If the Gods had not availed themselves of Ahriman's services in forming our bony head, we would be walking around with animal heads.

The divine powers also, however, make use of the luciferic spirits. If they did not do so, the extremities, or our limb system, would not be able to undergo a transformation from our present incarnation to the one that follows. For this the luciferic beings are necessary. We owe it to the luciferic beings that when we die the present form of our limbs is gradually transformed into the further form that belongs to the next incarnation. In the middle of the path between death and a new birth Ahriman then has to intervene in order to undertake the other task of re-moulding our head in the appropriate way. Just as we would be going about with animal heads if we did not have Ahriman to thank for providing us with human ones, our limb nature would not be meta-morphosed into its human aspect by the next incarnation but would instead take on a demonic aspect. We do in any event lose the head that we have now when we die, not merely as material substance which is united with the Earth but also in terms of its form; and we do indeed bring into our next incarnation what becomes head out of what is carried over from our limb system. But what is thus carried over would become demonic if we did not have the luciferic powers that are con-nected with us to thank that the transformation can take place from a demon of a purely soul-spiritual nature to the human form of the next incarnation.

So both ahrimanic and luciferic powers must cooperate in order for us to become human beings, and the essentially human aspect cannot be understood without taking into account the help given by both Ahriman and Lucifer. As regards its future, mankind cannot dispense with really understanding the influences of Ahriman and Lucifer. The Bible tells us with absolute justice that the God spoken of at the beginning of the biblical story breathed into man the living breath. But the living breath works within the trunk, or the middle system of man's being. Thus in so far as our concern is with those divine beings who work in a normal way, we are dealing only with this middle system. To the extent that we have to do with the human head, we are dealing with an opponent of the powers of Jehovah and, hence, also with an adversary of Christ; and to the extent that our concern is with man's limb system, we are dealing with the luciferic adversary.

So one will only understand man if one conceives of him in these three aspects. In the Group that is to stand at the focal point of our building[9] you therefore have this trinity of aspects: the Representative of Humanity, who is fashioned in such a way that here the forces of breathing, of the trunk, are given prominence, the activity of the heart and so forth. This is the central figure. Then there is that figure in which is active everything of a headlike nature, Ahriman, and that figure in which there works everything connected with the extremities or limbs, Lucifer.

One has to divide the being of man in this way if one is wanting to understand him, for in the individual human being man as such is united with Ahriman and Lucifer. At the same time this is indicative of the fact that everything that is more or less associated with human thinking, which is of course with respect to its physical context bound up with the head (human thinking is enacted on the basis of perceptions as a process associated with the outward senses), has an ahrimanic character. We perceive nature mainly through the senses of the head, and we form for ourselves a picture of nature with the ahrimanic character just described because we ourselves bear the ahrimanic principle in the way that our head has been formed.

Ideals, on the other hand, from the inner, psychological standpoint (I shall return to this on a subsequent occasion[10]) have a great deal to do with love, with everything that belongs to the extremities or the limb system. Because of this the luciferic power has a ready access to ideals. Ahriman takes hold of us through our head, Lucifer through our extremities. It is through our head that Ahriman deludes us into conceiving of nature as devoid of spirit; while through our limbs Lucifer misleads us into conceiving of ideals that lack any connection with the forces of the natural world.

The task of man today is to arrive at a true overview by seeing such things as a whole. You will then see that there is in us a certain barrier that divides us, and that this barrier is in the middle of our trunk, thus separating the head forces, which are ahrimanic in nature, from the luciferic forces, which belong to the limb system. If, through a mystical insight into our own being, we were able to look right through ourselves, we would indeed understand the natural order by means of our head but we would also gain insight into ourselves by means of the natural order. And if the luciferic powers in us were to have things their own way, they would also enlighten us about the ahrimanic powers, and we would in this way arrive at a connection between the natural order and the domain of spirit. But there is a particular reason why we cannot do this, and this is that we have a memory. Everything that we receive from nature by way of ideas, concepts and impressions we store up in our memory. And if this here [see Diagram 4] is a diagrammatic representation of the head region, if this represents the chest region and trunk and this the extremities or limbs, it is the dividing wall in the trunk region that leads to what we take in of the natural order by way of our head to return to us as the substance of memory. This is why we do not reach down in our perception to where the luciferic influence is active, and why we do not observe the ahrimanic influence, just as we do not see what is behind a mirror but only what is being reflected. Here the natural order is reflected in what separates the ahrimanic from the luciferic in us and is at the same time the basis for our memory, for the power of recollection that is thereby being formed. If we were unable to remember the things that we have experienced, if this dividing wall were not there, if in looking into ourselves we were to see right through, we would look right down to the luciferic influence in us, and we would also perceive the ahrimanic influence.

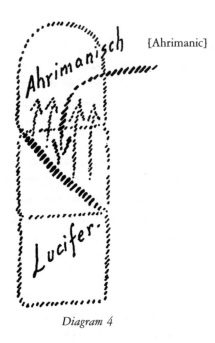

[Ahrimanic]

Diagram 4

But now consider for a moment. What we are shown in this mirror is precisely that which we live through in the course of life, and it is this that we look back upon after death, it is from out of this that a mobile or fluid ego becomes one that is firmly fixed. This is what we look back upon, this is what accompanies our life. And Ahriman and Lucifer work along with us, and in such a way that Ahriman enables us to bear a human head and Lucifer enables us to avoid becoming a demon, thus giving us the possibility of attaining a further incarnation.

I have been somewhat trying your patience with matters that are perhaps rather more difficult to understand, but I wanted to evoke at least a sense for the actual reason why the gulf between idealism and realism has arisen. It has arisen through the fact that Lucifer inspires us with idealism that is powerless in nature and that Ahriman calls forth within us a picture of the natural order which appears to us as utterly devoid of spirit. So the idealists, the abstract idealists, are under a luciferic influence, and materialists are under an ahrimanic influence. It is necessary that one should concern oneself with such things, that instead of adhering rigidly to a system in the name of theosophy one considers these matters in greater detail; for it is necessary that man becomes aware that he needs to put some energy into ensuring that he will be able to remain united with the spirit for the rest of earthly evolution. This is an uncomfortable truth, one might even say a hateful truth—hateful, because it runs counter to so much that people like, that they like because it suits them to do so. There could be no greater challenge for people today than to be told that if they want to retain their connection with the spirit they need to do something about it. Most people would prefer the Mystery of Golgotha to have occurred in order that they should not have to do anything about their situation, that their sins have been redeemed by Christ and they can go to heaven without any effort of their own. This is why most theologians are so incensed by anthroposophy, because of course from an anthroposophical standpoint it will never be acknowledged that there is nothing that man has to do in order to maintain his connection with the spirit, that in the future of earthly evolution this will simply proceed without any contribution on his part. The connection between the physical and the spiritual domains, between the members of man's being as they are between birth and death and between death and a new birth, is one that will be put into question in the course of future earthly evolution, and it will only avoid entering into a state of disorder if human beings are really able to concern themselves with the spirit with the future in mind. There is spiritual-scientific evidence for this today. This evidence contains *highly* uncomfortable truths, but they shed light on matters that are of the greatest importance and significance.

The connection between man's soul and spirit and his physical and etheric nature in the present has, I would say, already become very loose, and people today need to be increasingly awake lest something happens with respect to the connection between their physical and etheric bodies and the soul-spiritual aspects of their being that could lead to these latter aspects being as it were sucked out of them. For if prejudices such as that there is no need during life to know anything about how things will be after one's death become more and more pronounced, or if the gulf between so-called idealism and the purely natural order becomes ever wider, there is the danger of an increasing possibility of losing one's soul. There is today still a safeguard against this happening, in that when young people die the spiritual world is endowed with a certain gravity and Lucifer's calculations are upset, and when old people die so much spirituality is exuded into the physical world that Ahriman's calculations are put into disarray. But one should not forget that as human beings renounce their connection with the spiritual domain the ahrimanic and luciferic powers will become ever mightier and that gradually, as the Earth descends ever further into a state of devolution, this wall of defence will no longer be able to be fully effective.

What I should like to see is that a sort of basic theme should result from our studies in the form of a feeling—and feelings are always the most important aspect of what can arise from spiritual-scientific activity—for the need to give proper attention to spiritual matters from the present cycle of Earth evolution onwards. I have emphasized from a variety of different viewpoints that from our present time onwards human beings need to focus their attention on spiritual concerns. And the only way in which this can be achieved in times to come is that people really make the effort to understand and assimilate—as opposed to resist—even such difficult matters as we have been preoccupied with in the course of these days and especially today. There needs to be an understanding for the perspectivity of time. When people have arrived at an understanding of the perspectivity of time, they will no longer say: here is idealism, but it is only a dream which has no power to influence the natural world, and on the other hand is the natural order, but they will have come to recognize that the ideals that live within us are seeds for the future, and the natural order is the fruit of the past.

This sentence expresses a golden rule: every ideal is a seed for a future event in nature; every natural event is the fruit of a spiritual event in the past. Only by means of this rule can one find the bridge between idealism and realism. But something else is necessary if this is to happen. No ideal has ever existed or could ever be the seed for a future event in nature if this future event were to be prevented by what is happening in the natural world now. We can look at some such hypothesis. Let us consider the possibility, which indeed applies today, that through the so-called law of entropy earthly evolution enters into a state of general warming and that all other natural forces cease. In such an ultimate state such as this all ideals would of course fade into oblivion. Such an ultimate state is a natural consequence of the supposition that present physical conditions will continue purely in accordance with the law of causality. If one thinks on the lines of present-day physics that—according to the law of the conservation of energy and matter[11]—such an ultimate state will indeed arise, there is no place for an ideal to be absorbed into a natural event in the future, for any future event will simply be the consequence of a present event in nature. But this is not the case. Things are not what they appear to be according to the present conception of nature but can be viewed quite differently. Everything existing today as matter and energy will at a certain point in the future no longer be there. There is no such thing as a law of conservation of matter and energy. Where one seeks matter there is nothing other than the influence of a previous ahrimanic activity, and what surrounds us by way of the sense-perceptible world will after a certain time no longer exist. And if everything that is now of a physical nature is no longer there, if everything has been completely dissolved, the time will have come when present ideals in the form of natural occurrences will have been added to what is now being destroyed.

This is how it is in the wider universe. The situation for the human individual is that he will incarnate again in the next period of cosmic evolution, when the conditions in which he has lived during the present incarnation have to some extent been overcome, thus when an environment can be created for him that is different from the present one, when all that binds him now to the Earth has disappeared from the present environment. When everything has changed in such a way that he can experience something new, this is when he will reincarnate. The present ideals that can be formed in man will be nature once everything that is nature at present no longer exists and something new has arisen. But the new that arises is none other than the spirit that has become nature.

We must find the bridge over the abyss behind the natural phenomena and the ideals. This is what we need to discover. We can reach it today if we do not shrink from developing our concepts so forcefully that they are themselves able to become realities. Thus the need in our modern times is to enter fully into everything that can be learnt of a spiritual nature. But allow me to add that it will be most important for there to be an ever greater degree of open-mindedness with regard to spiritual matters. The day before yesterday I referred to what is hindering the growth of spiritual science specifically from within the Anthroposophical Society. Above all else a genuine open-mindedness needs ever and again to be cultivated in this realm. Time and again we experience that the disintegrative tendency that brought about materialism and led to the destruction of the old spirituality has also, by way of human thinking, pervaded the spiritual domain and specifically where spiritual aims are being pursued. I have already drawn attention to how materialistic a lot of theosophical conceptions can be. It is of course not easy when one is discussing matters of a spiritual-scientific nature to find the right words, because our language today is no longer suited to spiritual concepts and because we must once again seek a connection between language and what we want to convey that is appropriate for spiritual things. But it is necessary that we avoid damaging the anthroposophical movement by what is so especially harmful. We need to characterize matters of a spiritual nature in an open-minded way. Again and again I find myself being asked about people who, it is said, are having spiritual experiences. The essence of the questions that are frequently asked is: should one blindly accept the truth of what this or that person sees? If one responds affirmatively to the question, this gives rise to blind devotion; if one replies in the negative, what happens is that the person in question is immediately branded as a heretic and is told that his clairvoyance is atavistic and is therefore of no account. Well, this either-or way of dealing with these matters must really be transformed. We must approach statements about spiritual phenomena with a thoroughly healthy intelligence. But if we want to be dogmatic, we cannot be spiritual scientists. If we either idolize people or condemn them for heresy, we cannot become spiritual scientists. There will be infinite numbers of worthy contributions towards characterizing the spiritual world from quarters that one might not regard as absolutely reliable.

It may also happen that people start singing the praises of an individual with clairvoyant faculties. It may then transpire that this person has been glossing over a few things or even maybe quite a lot, and this individual is then strongly repudiated. The same people who formerly idolized him now reject him altogether.

Well, one cannot make any progress as human beings in this fashion. No progress is possible with this 'either-or' of adulating people or condemning them for heresy but only by approaching things with one's healthy human understanding. It may, for example, also happen that something wholly true, important and essential emerges from the spiritual world through someone whom one knows to be perfectly capable of telling outrageous lies.

One would not arrive at this 'either-or' situation to which I am referring if instead of introducing dogmatic ideas one endeavoured to work within this anthroposophical movement with one's healthy powers of reason. That is the one thing. The other is this, that because of the way that things are frequently dealt with in our circles it is extraordinarily difficult for the Anthroposophical Society to find its place in the cultural life of the present time. If this is to happen a certain discernment is required from those people who are involved with the Society; and those who are involved in it have a growing obligation to exercise such powers of discrimination. For the Anthroposophical Society will have completely lost its way if we do not try to form a connection with the wider cultural movements of our time, if we again and again fall into the error of practising sectarianism. It will be the death of our movement if we become sectarian. You need only think that the kind of things that we have been discussing in the course of these days would not be considered particularly strange by someone who is in the midst of the scientific and cultural life of the present time, provided that he were to approach them in a sufficiently unprejudiced way. But in order to accomplish anything of this sort the will to discriminate needs to be present. It easily happens that the question as to whether someone or other should be allowed to listen to anthroposophical lectures or be given one of the cycles to read is asked in a somewhat theoretical way, without taking into account the level of education or general circumstances of the person concerned. This theoretical approach does us a great deal of harm. It is responsible for the fact that a person such as the one in Holland around whom all manner of mischief has been crystallizing is able to drift into the Anthroposophical Society and find there people who protect him, whereas others who possess good judgement are often repelled by such conduct.

I shall now give you a specific instance. Some time ago Herr von Bernus[12] joined the Anthroposophical Society with the clear intention—the evaluation of which is open to anyone with a healthy human intelligence—of building a bridge between the wider cultural environment, the literary and scientific life of the present, and our anthroposophical life. Now, Herr von Bernus has, for example, in his own way recast a number of things that I have said both in my books and in my lectures in his own poetic style and published the result. He has himself shown me the pile of letters of complaint that he has received for having made what was for once a timely effort to carry out his intention! One can hardly be surprised if someone for whom I dare say much is at stake could well be repelled by such behaviour to which he was subjected then by the Anthroposophical Society. Nevertheless, the journal that he founded[13] will be of immense service to the anthroposophical movement. He also enabled the anthroposophical movement in Munich to be represented in his art gallery.[14] But one could observe a certain resistance to something that was both justified and possible! If one considers von Bernus's experiences as a whole, one has a true picture of what both the anthroposophical movement and the Anthroposophical Society need to learn in order to be a real Society.

To the extent that the building in Dornach has come into being, it *is* a Society. But much else has not been achieved, which plainly shows that the Anthroposophical Society does not regard itself as a Society but as a collection of separate little sectarian circles. We must really emerge from this stage of sectarianism; but we shall not be able to do so unless we give some serious thought to what we are trying to achieve.

It is so very difficult to say such things, and indeed one says them with great reluctance, but there is nevertheless much that is necessary for me to say because I am personally so strongly involved with this anthroposophical movement of ours. If the Anthroposophical Society is increasingly developing towards the point where it is becoming a Society with the explicit tendency of reducing me to silence—a tendency that is actually growing, and one that has always existed—it is not a matter of personal vanity if I emphasize this. I am most reluctant to have to say this, but the tendency towards reducing me to silence is one that is becoming a common feature in the Anthroposophical

Society, and so the personal element is interconnected with our practical concerns. Because the Society has not been behaving as a Society should, what has been rising to the surface like poisonous scum are the derogatory comments that lapsed members have been putting out into the world.

These are indeed matters that I sometimes have to point out and which cannot remain unspoken. I have alluded to them in places where I have been able to speak recently, because I firmly believe that in these tragic times much depends on anthroposophy being presented to the world in the right way. But it is so difficult to bring about some deeper reflection regarding the question: what can be done within the domain of anthroposophy to enable the Anthroposophical Society to become a real Society? Initial efforts are indeed being made by certain individuals, but generally speaking nothing gets beyond these early beginnings. But now that I have drawn attention once more to these matters, I would hope that some further thought can be given to them. I say this not for personal reasons but out of the necessities of the times, just as from what I have presented in the course of these days you will be able to derive some fruitful ideas which can help you to understand the catastrophic times in which we are living.

[Words written on the blackboard]   2 September 1918

Every ideal is a seed for a future event in nature.

Every natural event is the fruit of a spiritual event in the past.

NOTES TO THIS EDITION

Source of the text: The lectures were taken down in shorthand by Helene Finckh (1883–1960). The present publication is based on her notes.

The first edition in book form, edited with notes by Johann Waeger and Robert Friedenthal, was published in 1967 as part of the Collected Works (Gesamtausgabe). *The second edition (1990)* was revised by Susi Lötscher. Some corrections based on a comparison with the original shorthand text and also some minor stylistic alterations needed to be made at various points. An index of names has been added. The detailed summaries of the lectures made by Marie Steiner for the edition of 1940 have again been included.

The title of the volume derives from Marie Steiner.

The blackboard drawings for these lectures have not been preserved. However, Helene Finckh recorded the drawings in the shorthand text, and on the basis of these drafts Assya Turgeniev (1890–1966) was able to re-draw them by means of the sketching technique that she had developed.

Separate editions: The first edition of *Die Wissenschaft vom Werden des Menschen*, published by Marie Steiner in Dornach in 1940, appeared in three volumes: 1. *Okkulte Psychologie* (Lectures 1–3), 2. *Die Geheimnisse der Sonne und des dreigeteilten Menschen* (Lectures 4–6) and 3. *Das Walten der kosmischen Vernunft im Sprachentstehen. Die todbringende und geistweckende Weltenkraft der Hierarchien* (Lectures 7–9). The lectures have never been published in English, although translations of the three parts of the cycle as detailed above exist in typescript form under the respective titles: 'Occult Psychology' (Typescript Z 253), 'The Mysteries of the Sun and of Threefold Man' (Typescript Z 254) and 'The Ruling of Cosmic Intelligence present in Speech Formation' (Typescript Z 271).

Lecture 1

1. See the lecture with slides given on 29 June 1921 in Bern entitled 'The Architectural Conception of the Goetheanum'. Planned for inclusion in GA 289.
2. Dr Steiner had last spoken to the members in Dornach on 17 January 1918, so he had been away for seven months.
3. The Anthroposophical Society was founded on 28 December 1912 in Cologne, on separating from the Theosophical Society. See *The Anthroposophic Movement*, a cycle of 8 lectures given in Dornach in June 1923 (GA 258).
4. The wooden Group, *The Representative of Humanity*, portraying Christ between Lucifer and Ahriman.

5. The lectures referred to here are two given in Munich on 15 and 17 February 1918 under the title *Das Sinnlich-Übersinnliche in seiner Verwirklichung durch die Kunst* (that of 15 February is included in *Art as Spiritual Activity*) and two further lectures given in the same city on 5 and 6 May 1918 entitled *Die Quellen der künstlerischen Phantasie und die Quellen der übersinnlichen Erkenntnis* (the second of which is available in Typescript Z 186, *Sources of Artistic Imagination and the Sources of Supersensible Knowledge*). All these lectures are included in GA 271.

6. Alexander Freiherr von Bernus (1880–1963), poet. From 1916 until 1921 he published the quarterly journal *Das Reich* in Munich. Rudolf Steiner occasionally gave his Munich lectures in his art centre.

7. Woodrow Wilson (1856–1924), President of the USA from 1912 until 1920. On 8 January 1918 he proclaimed a peace programme to Congress in the form of his 'Fourteen Points'.

8. George Santayana (1863–1952), American philosopher of Spanish descent. Came to America in 1872, where he remained until 1912. His book *Egotism in German Philosophy* (1916) appeared in a French edition entitled *L'érreur de la philosophie allemande* (Paris 1917) with a foreword by Emile Boutroux (see note 10 below). See especially its fourth chapter, 'Tendancés à l'égotisme dans Goethe', pp. 61 ff., and especially from p. 69.

9. Between 1909 and 1917 Theobald von Bethman Hollweg had been the Imperial Chancellor of Germany.

10. Emile Boutroux (1845–1921), French philosopher. See note 8 above.

11. This is a reference to earlier evolutionary conditions of the Earth planet, not to the heavenly bodies with these names. See Rudolf Steiner, *An Outline of Occult Science* (GA 13), the chapter entitled 'The Evolution of the World and Man'.

12. *Anthroposophie und akademische Wissenschaft*, 4 lectures given between 5 and 14 November 1917 (GA 73). English translation published under the title *Anthroposophy has Something to Add to Modern Sciences*. Oscar Hertwig's book (see note 13 below) is referred to by Rudolf Steiner in the lecture of 12 November ('Anthroposophy and Natural Science').

13. Oscar Hertwig (1849–1922), anatomist and biologist. The book mentioned here, *Das Werden der Organismen. Eine Widerlegung von Darwin's Zufallstheorie*, was published in Jena in 1916.

14. Oscar Hertwig, *Zur Abwehr des ethischen, des sozialen, des politischen Darwinismus* ('A Defence against Ethical, Social and Political Darwinism'), Jena 1918.

15. Regarding these so-called 'Begabtenprüfungen' see, for example, Ernst Meumann, *Vorlesungen zur Einführung in die experimentelle Pädagogik und ihre psychologischen Grundlagen* ('Lectures on an Introduction to an Experimental Approach to the Theory and Methodology of Education and its Psychological Foundations'), 3 volumes 1907, second edition Leipzig 1911–14: vol. 1, lecture 4, esp. pp. 324 f and vol. 2, lecture 10, esp. pp. 264 f and lecture 11, esp. pp. 444 f.

16. Hermann von Helmholtz (1821–94), physiologist and physicist. Inventor of the ophthalmoscope (1851).

17. Isaac Newton (1642–1727), English scientist, mathematician and astron-

omer. Founder of classical theoretical physics and of a mechanistic conception of the cosmos.

18. Woodrow Wilson, *The New Freedom* (1913), German translation published in 1914. His book on literature (1893) includes his essay on 'The Course of American History'. A German translation appeared in 1913.

19. Herman Grimm (1828–1901), a specialist in aesthetics and literary studies. See also Rudolf Steiner's autobiography *The Course of My Life* (GA 28).

20. See note 14.

21. Herbert Spencer (1820–1903), English philosopher.

22. John Stuart Mill (1806–73), English philosopher and economist. A founder of positivism and one of the main advocates of modern empiricism.

23. Henri Bergson (1859–1941), French philosopher.

24. Alexander III (1845–94), Russian Tsar.

25. Vladimir Ilich Lenin (real name Ulyanov) (1870–1924), was the leader of the Bolshevik Revolution in 1917.

26. Karl Marx (1818–83). Founder of scientific socialism and co-author of the *Communist Manifesto* (1848).

Lecture 2

1. *Theosophy. An Introduction to the Supersensible Knowledge of the World and the Destination of Man* (1904), GA 9 and *An Outline of Occult Science*, GA 13.

2. 'Ignorabimus': an expression of the Berlin physiologist Emil Dubois-Reymond (1818–96) in his lecture at the second open meeting of the 45th Assembly of German Scientists and Doctors in Leipzig on 14 August 1872: 'Über die Grenzen des Naturerkennens' (On the Limits of Natural Science). What he actually said was this: 'With regard to the riddle of the bodily world scientists have long accustomed themselves to give expression with a manly sense of acceptance to their "ignorabimus". As they look back at what has been successfully undertaken they are carried by the quiet awareness that where they know nothing they could at least have some knowledge under certain circumstances and one day perhaps will. But with respect to the riddle of the nature of matter and force and how one might conceive of them, they are obliged for ever to make the far harder resolve to admit: "Ignorabimus!" '

3. In the words of another quotation from the same lecture by Dubois-Reymond: 'We shall never know better than we do today that, as Paul Erman was accustomed to say, "here" where matter resides "space is haunted".'

4. Rudolf Steiner is probably referring here to the lecture of 27 February 1917 in *Cosmic and Human Metamorphoses* (one of 17 lectures given in Berlin included in GA 175).

5. A quotation from Schiller's poem *Der Taucher*.

6. See note 4 to Lecture 1.

Lecture 3

1. See, for example, the lecture of 25 June 1918 given in Berlin (GA 181). An English translation is available in Typescript C 50, 'A Sound Outlook for Today'.

2. In the lecture of 29 July 1916 in Dornach (GA 170), *The Riddle of Humanity*.

3. Otto Weininger (1880–1903), Austrian philosopher. New editions of both books referred to were published in Leipzig in 1918.
4. 'It is probably impossible to have any memory of our condition before birth because we entered so deeply into oblivion through being born: we lost consciousness and demanded impulsively to be born, without knowledge or rational resolve, and therefore we know absolutely nothing about this past' (aphorism no. 2 from *Über die letzten Dinge*, 4th edition Vienna and Leipzig 1918).
5. 'I am killing myself so that I do not have to murder another person' (from the same book, p. 190).
6. Rabindranath Tagore (1861–1941), Indian poet and philosopher.
7. 'The Course of American History', see note 18 to Lecture 1.
8. Much can be found on this theme in the writings of William Morris and John Ruskin. See, for example, *News from Nowhere and Other Writings*, Penguin Books 1993/2004, especially the lecture entitled 'The Hopes of Civilization', and *Unto This Last*.
9. See Rudolf Steiner, *An Outline of Occult Science* (1910), GA 13.
10. See Rudolf Steiner, *Christianity as Mystical Fact and the Mysteries of Antiquity* (1902), GA 8.
11. Otto Zimmermann SJ, 'Anthroposophische Irrlehren', *Stimmen der Zeit*, 48th year, vol. 95, no. 10, July 1918, pp. 328 f.; Joseph Kreitmaier SJ, 'Vom Expressionismus', ibid. pp. 356 f.

Lecture 4
1. This refers to Plato (427–347 BC), philosopher, pupil of Socrates. See especially his *Politeia* ('Politics'), book 6, 508a–509b.
2. Arthur Balfour (1848–1930) was British Foreign Secretary between 1916 and 1919.
3. 1855–1927.
4. See Lecture 7 in this volume (31 August 1918), note 2.
5. Cf. Rudolf Steiner's books *Cosmic Memory* (1904), GA 11, and *An Outline of Occult Science* (1910), GA 13.
6. Cf. Mark 13:31.

Lecture 5
1. See note 5 to Lecture 4.
2. This was the lecture given on 23 May 1916 in Berlin (GA 167). An English translation can be found as part of the cycle of lectures in Typescript C 42, 'Things of the Present and of the Past in the Spirit of Man' and in Typescript Z 243, 'A Fragment from the Jewish Haggada'.
3. See the lecture of 14 October 1917 given in Dornach (GA 177), *The Fall of the Spirits of Darkness*.
4. See note 11 to Lecture 1.
5. See Lecture 2 (18 August 1918), Diagram 2.
6. See Diagram 2, Lecture 2.
7. See *The Case for Anthroposophy*, extracts from *Von Seelenrätseln* (1917), GA 21, section VIII, 'The Real Basis of Intentional Relation'. See also *Riddles of the Soul*, Mercury Press 1999.

8. Bjørnstjerne Bjørnson (1832–1910), Norwegian playwright, novelist and poet.

9. Nero reigned from AD 54 until 68.

10. Reigned AD 69–79.

11. Reigned AD 79–81.

12. Reigned AD 81–96.

13. Reigned AD 96–98.

14. AD 70–140, Roman historian who wrote biographies of the Caesars.

15. AD *c*. 55–*c*. 120, Roman historian.

16. Flavius P. Philostratus the Elder, Greek sophist at the end of the second century AD. Described the life of Apollonius of Tyana.

17. Apollonius of Tyana, prophet and miracle-worker in the first century AD.

18. Ferdinand Christian Baur (1792–1860), Protestant theologian. *Apollonius von Tyana und Christus*, Tübingen 1832.

Lecture 6

1. See the earlier note concerning Plato.

2. See *Theosophy*, ch. III, section one, 'The Soul-world'.

3. See Goethe, *Die Metamorphose der Pflanzen* ('The Metamorphosis of Plants'), in Goethe: *Naturwissenschaftliche Schriften* ('Scientific Writings'), edited and with a commentary by Rudolf Steiner in Kürschner's *Deutsche National-Literatur*, 5 vols (1884–97, Dornach edition 1975, GA 1a–e vol. 1 GA 1a, pp. 17 f and Rudolf Steiner's introduction in the same volume.

4. Ibid.

5. See Lecture 9 (2 September 1918) in this volume.

6. For example in *Universe, Earth and Man in their Relationship to Egyptian Myths and Modern Civilization*, 11 lectures, Stuttgart 1908 (GA 105); *Egyptian Myths and Mysteries*, 12 lectures, Leipzig 1908 (GA 106).

7. 63 BC–AD 14, first Roman Emperor, Caesar Augustus.

8. The essay entitled *Die Chymische Hochzeit des Christian Rosenkreutz* appeared in the quarterly *Das Reich*, published by Alexander von Bernus in Munich, in three parts between October 1917 and April 1918. It is included in GA 35. An English translation is available.

9. Johann Valentin Andreae (1586–1654), Lutheran pastor in Württemberg, and writer.

10. Published in Kassel in 1614. This work ascribed to Johann Valentin Andreae is said to have been a translation of a publication by the Italian, Boccalini.

11. Compare Rudolf Steiner's reference to this movement in his autobiography, *The Course of My Life*, 1923–5 (GA 28), ch. XVII.

12. 'Eine "Gesellschaft für ethische Kultur"', included in GA 31, *Gesammelte Aufsätze zur Kultur- und Zeitgeschichte 1887–1901*. (Cf. also the article entitled 'Eine "Gesellschaft für ethische Kultur in Deutschland"', ibid., pp. 164 f.) This article brought Harden a flood of enraged letters in which Rudolf Steiner was attacked 'in a hateful manner'. See in this connection his letters to Pauline Specht (of 3 December 1892) and to Ernst Haeckel (of 4 December 1892) in *Briefe, vol. 2 1890–1925* (GA 39), letters nos 340 and 341. Rudolf Steiner's reply to these devastating criticisms, 'Alte und neue Moralbegriffe' ('Old and

New Moral Concepts'), appeared in a later issue of *Die Zukunft*. (Printed in the volume of articles and essays referred to, pp. 180 f.)

13. A weekly journal edited by Maximilian Harden (whose real name was Witkowski), 1891–1927.

14. Rudolf Steiner refers to this conversation in *The Course of My Life*, ch. XVII.

15. This is referred to in the lecture of 14 April 1914 in Vienna (GA 153), included in the volume *The Inner Nature of Man and Our Life between Death and a New Birth*.

16. See Lecture 1.

17. Ibid.

18. Ferdinand Lassalle (1825–64), socialist leader.

19. Eduard Bernstein (1850–1932), socialist theoretician, founder of revisionism.

20. The German word used here refers to the official seats of the highest Roman dignitaries.

Lecture 7

1. Carl Freiherr du Prel (1839–99), a writer of books on occult philosophy. *Das Rätsel des Menschen. Einleitung in das Studium der Geheimwissenschaften*, Leipzig 1892. See also *Der Spiritismus*, 1886 and *Ein Wort über Spiritismus*, 1887.

2. See Lecture 4 (24 August 1918) in this volume and also the following note.

3. Julius Robert Mayer (1814–78), doctor and scientist, put forward the law of the conservation of energy and matter with the paper entitled 'Bemerkungen über die Kräfte in der unbelebten Natur' ('Observations Regarding Forces in Inanimate Nature'), in *Liebigs Annalen*, Heidelberg, vol. 42, no. 2, pp. 233–40. See also: *Robert Mayer über die Erhaltung der Kraft* ('Robert Mayer on the Conservation of Energy'), four treatises, edited and with a commentary by A. Neuberger, Leipzig (no date). Compare Rudolf Steiner's lecture of 16 April 1918 (GA 181), one of 21 lectures given in Berlin (see Typescript C 49, 'Anthroposophical Life-Gifts'), where he says among other things: '... But this idea did not become generally known in the highly refined form in which Mayer presented it but in a much coarser way. This derives from the fact that it was not the thoughts of Julius Robert Mayer that were adopted by science but those of the English brewer, Joule and the physicist Helmholtz.'

4. Johann Gutenberg (real name J. Gensfleisch, 1394–1468). Around 1445 he invented movable printing types.

5. *Philosophie und Anthroposophie* first appeared in 1908 under the title *Philosophie und Theosophie*, in accordance with the shorthand notes of a lecture for members given in Stuttgart on 17 August 1908. For the 1918 edition Rudolf Steiner completely reworked the text of the lecture notes and changed the title to *Philosophie und Anthroposophie*. The essay is included in GA 35, and exists in an English translation under the title given in the main text.

6. See note 4 to Lecture 1.

7. For example, on 29 October 1917 ('On Changes in the Conception of Christ', Typescript Z 173), GA 292.

8. See Rudolf Steiner, *The Riddles of Philosophy, Presented in an Outline of Its History* (1914), GA 18.

9. Pythagoras (*c.* 582–497 BC), Greek philosopher and mathematician.

10. This story can be found in Plutarch in *On Isis and Osiris*, ch. 12 (*Moral Writings*, vol. 5).
11. Plutarch (*c.* 45–*c.* 125), Greek philosopher and historian, names the priest Oinuphis of Heliopolis as the teacher of Pythagoras.
12. Jakob Böhme (1575–1624), Protestant mystic and philosopher. *De Signatura Rerum or: Concerning the Birth and Designation of All Beings*, 'written in 1622 and printed in the year of the great salvation, 1730'.
13. Max Müller (1823–1900), researcher in Sanskrit and religion at Oxford.
14. Charles Darwin (1809–82), English scientist.
15. Ernst Haeckel (1834–1919), German philosopher, zoologist.
16. This restriction was lifted at the Christmas Conference in 1923/1924.

Lecture 8
1. Apollonius of Tyana.
2, J[Y]ehovah (v = u).
3. See observation about the blackboard drawings in the notes to this edition.
4. Sybaris was a town in Lower Italy, founded in 700 BC, proverbial for the opulence of its inhabitants.

Lecture 9
1. Immanuel Kant (1724–1804), philosopher, mathematician and scientist. The reference is to Kant's *Critique of Pure Reason*. See, for example, Andrew Ward, *Kant: The Three Critiques* (Cambridge, 2006).
2. Robert Zimmermann (1824–98), aesthete and philosopher. *Anthroposophie im Umriss*, Vienna 1882, pp. 307 f.
3. Auguste Comte (1798–1857), French philosopher. Founder of positivism and sociology. *Système de Politique Positive ou Traité de Sociologie instituant de la Réligion de l'Humanité*, 4 vols., Paris 1851–4. *Cours de Philosophie Positive*, 6 vols., Paris 1830–42.
4. Friedrich Schiller (1759–1805). *Briefe über die ästhetische Erziehung des Menschen* (1795), 22nd letter.
5. Friedrich Schleiermacher (1768–1834), Evangelical theologian, preacher and philosopher. *Grundlinien einer Kritik der bisherigen Sittenlehre* (1803), section 50.
6. Robert Zimmermann, *Anthroposophie im Umriss*, Vienna 1882, p. 308.
7. GA 21 (1917). See (in English) *The Case for Anthroposophy*, ch. VII, 'The Principles of Psychosomatic Physiology'. See also *Riddles of the Soul*, Mercury Press 1999.
8. *Geheime Figuren der Rosenkreuzer aus dem sechzehnten und siebzehnten Jahrhundert*, 3 vols, Altona 1785–8 (anonymous). Volume 1 contains a treatise by Hinricus Madathanus Theosophus entitled *Aureum Seculum Redivivum*, which had appeared already in 1621. See in this connection Rudolf Steiner's two lectures of 27 and 28 September 1911 in Neuchâtel on Rosicrucian Christianity in *Esoteric Christianity*, 23 lectures in various towns in 1911–12 (GA 130).
9. See note 4 to Lecture 1.
10. See the lectures that followed this cycle entitled *Die Polarität von Dauer und Entwickelung im Menschenleben. Die kosmische Vorgeschichte der Menschheit*, 15 lectures given in Dornach between 6 September and 13 October 1918 (GA

184). Most of these lectures exist in English translations, although not currently as a single volume.

11. See note 3 to Lecture 7.
12. See note 6 to Lecture 1.
13. Ibid.
14. Ibid.

RUDOLF STEINER'S COLLECTED WORKS

The German Edition of Rudolf Steiner's Collected Works (the *Gesamtausgabe* [GA] published by Rudolf Steiner Verlag, Dornach, Switzerland) presently runs to 354 titles, organized either by type of work (written or spoken), chronology, audience (public or other), or subject (education, art, etc.). For ease of comparison, the Collected Works in English [CW] follows the German organization exactly. A complete listing of the CWs follows with literal translations of the German titles. Other than in the case of the books published in his lifetime, titles were rarely given by Rudolf Steiner himself, and were often provided by the editors of the German editions. The titles in English are not necessarily the same as the German; and, indeed, over the past seventy-five years have frequently been different, with the same book sometimes appearing under different titles.

For ease of identification and to avoid confusion, we suggest that readers looking for a title should do so by CW number. Because the work of creating the Collected Works of Rudolf Steiner is an ongoing process, with new titles being published every year, we have not indicated in this listing which books are presently available. To find out what titles in the Collected Works are currently in print, please check our website at www.rudolfsteinerpress.com (or www.steinerbooks.org for US readers).

Written Work

Public Lectures

CW 51	On Philosophy, History and Literature
CW 52	Spiritual Teachings Concerning the Soul and Observation of the World
CW 53	The Origin and Goal of the Human Being
CW 54	The Riddles of the World and Anthroposophy
CW 55	Knowledge of the Supersensible in Our Times and Its Meaning for Life Today
CW 56	Knowledge of the Soul and of the Spirit
CW 57	Where and How Does One Find the Spirit?
CW 58	The Metamorphoses of the Soul Life. Paths of Soul Experiences: Part One
CW 59	The Metamorphoses of the Soul Life. Paths of Soul Experiences: Part Two
CW 60	The Answers of Spiritual Science to the Biggest Questions of Existence
CW 61	Human History in the Light of Spiritual Research
CW 62	Results of Spiritual Research
CW 63	Spiritual Science as a Treasure for Life
CW 64	Out of Destiny-Burdened Times
CW 65	Out of Central European Spiritual Life
CW 66	Spirit and Matter, Life and Death
CW 67	The Eternal in the Human Soul. Immortality and Freedom
CW 68	Public lectures in various cities, 1906–1918
CW 69	Public lectures in various cities, 1906–1918
CW 70	Public lectures in various cities, 1906–1918
CW 71	Public lectures in various cities, 1906–1918
CW 72	Freedom—Immortality—Social Life
CW 73	The Supplementing of the Modern Sciences through Anthroposophy
CW 73a	Specialized Fields of Knowledge and Anthroposophy
CW 74	The Philosophy of Thomas Aquinas
CW 75	Public lectures in various cities, 1906–1918
CW 76	The Fructifying Effect of Anthroposophy on Specialized Fields
CW 77a	The Task of Anthroposophy in Relation to Science and Life: The Darmstadt College Course
CW 77b	Art and Anthroposophy. The Goetheanum-Impulse
CW 78	Anthroposophy, Its Roots of Knowledge and Fruits for Life
CW 79	The Reality of the Higher Worlds
CW 80	Public lectures in various cities, 1922
CW 81	Renewal-Impulses for Culture and Science—Berlin College Course
CW 82	So that the Human Being Can Become a Complete Human Being
CW 83	Western and Eastern World-Contrast. Paths to Understanding It through Anthroposophy
CW 84	What Did the Goetheanum Intend and What Should Anthroposophy Do?

Lectures to the Members of the Anthroposophical Society

SIGNIFICANT EVENTS IN THE LIFE OF RUDOLF STEINER

1829:   June 23: birth of Johann Steiner (1829–1910)—Rudolf Steiner's father—in Geras, Lower Austria.

1834:   May 8: birth of Franciska Blie (1834–1918)—Rudolf Steiner's mother—in Horn, Lower Austria. 'My father and mother were both children of the glorious Lower Austrian forest district north of the Danube.'

1860:   May 16: marriage of Johann Steiner and Franciska Blie.

1861:   February 25: birth of *Rudolf Joseph Lorenz Steiner* in Kraljevec, Croatia, near the border with Hungary, where Johann Steiner works as a telegrapher for the South Austria Railroad. Rudolf Steiner is baptized two days later, February 27, the date usually given as his birthday.

1862:   Summer: the family moves to Mödling, Lower Austria.

1863:   The family moves to Pottschach, Lower Austria, near the Styrian border, where Johann Steiner becomes stationmaster. 'The view stretched to the mountains ... majestic peaks in the distance and the sweet charm of nature in the immediate surroundings.'

1864:   November 15: birth of Rudolf Steiner's sister, Leopoldine (d. November 1, 1927). She will become a seamstress and live with her parents for the rest of her life.

1866:   July 28: birth of Rudolf Steiner's deaf-mute brother, Gustav (d. May 1, 1941).

1867:   Rudolf Steiner enters the village school. Following a disagreement between his father and the schoolmaster, whose wife falsely accused the boy of causing a commotion, Rudolf Steiner is taken out of school and taught at home.

1868:   A critical experience. Unknown to the family, an aunt dies in a distant town. Sitting in the station waiting room, Rudolf Steiner sees her 'form,' which speaks to him, asking for help. 'Beginning with this experience, a new soul life began in the boy, one in which not only the outer trees and mountains spoke to him, but also the worlds that lay behind them. From this moment on, the boy began to live with the spirits of nature...'

1869:   The family moves to the peaceful, rural village of Neudörfl, near Wiener-Neustadt in present-day Austria. Rudolf Steiner attends the village school. Because of the 'unorthodoxy' of his writing and spelling, he has to do 'extra lessons'.

1870:   Through a book lent to him by his tutor, he discovers geometry: 'To grasp something purely in the spirit brought me inner happiness. I know that I first learned happiness through geometry.' The same tutor allows him to draw, while other students still struggle with their reading and writing. 'An artistic element' thus enters his education.

1871:   Though his parents are not religious, Rudolf Steiner becomes a 'church child,' a favourite of the priest, who was 'an exceptional character'. 'Up to the age of ten or eleven, among those I came to know, he was far and away the most significant.' Among other things, he introduces Steiner to Copernican, heliocentric cosmology. As an altar boy, Rudolf Steiner serves at Masses, funerals, and Corpus Christi processions. At year's end, after an incident in which he escapes a thrashing, his father forbids him to go to church.

1872:   Rudolf Steiner transfers to grammar school in Wiener-Neustadt, a five-mile walk from home, which must be done in all weathers.

1873–75: Through his teachers and on his own, Rudolf Steiner has many wonderful experiences with science and mathematics. Outside school, he teaches himself analytic geometry, trigonometry, differential equations, and calculus.

1876:   Rudolf Steiner begins tutoring other students. He learns bookbinding from his father. He also teaches himself stenography.

1877:   Rudolf Steiner discovers Kant's *Critique of Pure Reason*, which he reads and rereads. He also discovers and reads von Rotteck's *World History*.

1878:   He studies extensively in contemporary psychology and philosophy.

1879:   Rudolf Steiner graduates from high school with honours. His father is transferred to Inzersdorf, near Vienna. He uses his first visit to Vienna 'to purchase a great number of philosophy books'—Kant, Fichte, Schelling, and Hegel, as well as numerous histories of philosophy. His aim: to find a path from the 'I' to nature.

October 1879–1883: Rudolf Steiner attends the Technical College in Vienna—to study mathematics, chemistry, physics, mineralogy, botany, zoology, biology, geology, and mechanics—with a scholarship. He also attends lectures in history and literature, while avidly reading philosophy on his own. His two favourite professors are Karl Julius Schröer (German language and literature) and Edmund Reitlinger (physics). He also audits lectures by Robert Zimmermann on aesthetics and Franz Brentano on philosophy. During this year he begins his friendship with Moritz Zitter (1861–1921), who will help support him financially when he is in Berlin.

1880:   Rudolf Steiner attends lectures on Schiller and Goethe by Karl Julius Schröer, who becomes his mentor. Also 'through a remarkable combination of circumstances,' he meets Felix Koguzki, a 'herb gatherer' and healer, who could 'see deeply into the secrets of nature'. Rudolf Steiner will meet and study with this 'emissary of the Master' throughout his time in Vienna.

1881:   January: '... I didn't sleep a wink. I was busy with philosophical problems until about 12:30 a.m. Then, finally, I threw myself down on my couch. All my striving during the previous year had been to research whether the following statement by Schelling was true or not: *Within everyone dwells a secret, marvelous capacity to draw back from the stream of time—out of the self clothed in all that comes to us from outside—into our innermost being and there, in the immutable form of the Eternal, to look into ourselves.* I believe, and I am still quite certain of it, that I discovered this capacity in myself; I had long had an inkling of it. Now the whole of idealist philosophy stood before me in modified form. What's a sleepless night compared to that!'

Rudolf Steiner begins communicating with leading thinkers of the day, who send him books in return, which he reads eagerly.

July: 'I am not one of those who dives into the day like an animal in human form. I pursue a quite specific goal, an idealistic aim—knowledge of the truth! This cannot be done offhandedly. It requires the greatest striving in the world, free of all egotism, and equally of all resignation.'

August: Steiner puts down on paper for the first time thoughts for a 'Philosophy of Freedom'. 'The striving for the absolute: this human yearning is freedom.' He also seeks to outline a 'peasant philosophy,' describing what the worldview of a 'peasant'—one who lives close to the earth and the old ways—really is.

1881–1882: Felix Koguzki, the herb gatherer, reveals himself to be the envoy of another, higher initiatory personality, who instructs Rudolf Steiner to penetrate Fichte's philosophy and to master modern scientific thinking as a preparation for right entry into the spirit. This 'Master' also teaches him the double (evolutionary and involutionary) nature of time.

1882:   Through the offices of Karl Julius Schröer, Rudolf Steiner is asked by Joseph Kürschner to edit Goethe's scientific works for the *Deutschen National-Literatur* edition. He writes 'A Possible Critique of Atomistic Concepts' and sends it to Friedrich Theodore Vischer.

1883:   Rudolf Steiner completes his college studies and begins work on the Goethe project.

1884:   First volume of Goethe's *Scientific Writings* (CW 1) appears (March). He lectures on Goethe and Lessing, and Goethe's approach to science. In July, he enters the household of Ladislaus and Pauline Specht as tutor to the four Specht boys. He will live there until 1890. At this time, he meets Josef Breuer (1842–1925), the co-author with Sigmund Freud of *Studies in Hysteria*, who is the Specht family doctor.

1885:   While continuing to edit Goethe's writings, Rudolf Steiner reads deeply in contemporary philosophy (Edouard von Hartmann, Johannes Volkelt, and Richard Wahle, among others).

1886:   May: Rudolf Steiner sends Kürschner the manuscript of *Outlines of Goethe's Theory of Knowledge* (CW 2), which appears in October, and which he sends out widely. He also meets the poet Marie Eugenie Delle Grazie and writes 'Nature and Our Ideals' for her. He attends her salon, where he meets many priests, theologians, and philosophers, who will become his friends. Meanwhile, the director of the Goethe Archive in Weimar requests his collaboration with the *Sophien* edition of Goethe's works, particularly the writings on colour.

1887:   At the beginning of the year, Rudolf Steiner is very sick. As the year progresses and his health improves, he becomes increasingly 'a man of letters,' lecturing, writing essays, and taking part in Austrian cultural life. In August–September, the second volume of Goethe's *Scientific Writings* appears.

1888: January–July: Rudolf Steiner assumes editorship of the 'German Weekly' (*Deutsche Wochenschrift*). He begins lecturing more intensively, giving, for example, a lecture titled 'Goethe as Father of a New Aesthetics'. He meets and becomes soul friends with Friedrich Eckstein (1861–1939), a vegetarian, philosopher of symbolism, alchemist, and musician, who will introduce him to various spiritual currents (including Theosophy) and with whom he will meditate and interpret esoteric and alchemical texts.

1889: Rudolf Steiner first reads Nietzsche (*Beyond Good and Evil*). He encounters Theosophy again and learns of Madame Blavatsky in the Theosophical circle around Marie Lang (1858–1934). Here he also meets well-known figures of Austrian life, as well as esoteric figures like the occultist Franz Hartmann and Karl Leinigen-Billigen (translator of C.G. Harrison's *The Transcendental Universe*). During this period, Steiner first reads A.P. Sinnett's *Esoteric Buddhism* and Mabel Collins's *Light on the Path*. He also begins travelling, visiting Budapest, Weimar, and Berlin (where he meets philosopher Edouard von Hartmann).

1890: Rudolf Steiner finishes volume 3 of Goethe's scientific writings. He begins his doctoral dissertation, which will become *Truth and Science* (CW 3). He also meets the poet and feminist Rosa Mayreder (1858–1938), with whom he can exchange his most intimate thoughts. In September, Rudolf Steiner moves to Weimar to work in the Goethe-Schiller Archive.

1891: Volume 3 of the Kürschner edition of Goethe appears. Meanwhile, Rudolf Steiner edits Goethe's studies in mineralogy and scientific writings for the *Sophien* edition. He meets Ludwig Laistner of the Cotta Publishing Company, who asks for a book on the basic question of metaphysics. From this will result, ultimately, *The Philosophy of Freedom* (CW 4), which will be published not by Cotta but by Emil Felber. In October, Rudolf Steiner takes the oral exam for a doctorate in philosophy, mathematics, and mechanics at Rostock University, receiving his doctorate on the twenty-sixth. In November, he gives his first lecture on Goethe's 'Fairy Tale' in Vienna.

1892: Rudolf Steiner continues work at the Goethe-Schiller Archive and on his *Philosophy of Freedom*. *Truth and Science*, his doctoral dissertation, is published. Steiner undertakes to write introductions to books on Schopenhauer and Jean Paul for Cotta. At year's end, he finds lodging with Anna Eunike, née Schulz (1853–1911), a widow with four daughters and a son. He also develops a friendship with Otto Erich Hartleben (1864–1905) with whom he shares literary interests.

1893: Rudolf Steiner begins his habit of producing many reviews and articles. In March, he gives a lecture titled 'Hypnotism, with Reference to Spiritism'. In September, volume 4 of the Kürschner edition is completed. In November, *The Philosophy of Freedom* appears. This year, too, he meets John Henry Mackay (1864–1933), the anarchist, and Max Stirner, a scholar and biographer.

1894: Rudolf Steiner meets Elisabeth Förster Nietzsche, the philosopher's sister, and begins to read Nietzsche in earnest, beginning with the as yet unpublished *Antichrist*. He also meets Ernst Haeckel (1834–1919). In the fall, he begins to write *Nietzsche, A Fighter against His Time* (CW 5).

1895: May, *Nietzsche, A Fighter against His Time* appears.

1896: January 22: Rudolf Steiner sees Friedrich Nietzsche for the first and only time. Moves between the Nietzsche and the Goethe-Schiller Archives, where he completes his work before year's end. He falls out with Elisabeth Förster Nietzsche, thus ending his association with the Nietzsche Archive.

1897: Rudolf Steiner finishes the manuscript of *Goethe's Worldview* (CW 6). He moves to Berlin with Anna Eunike and begins editorship of the *Magazin für Literatur*. From now on, Steiner will write countless reviews, literary and philosophical articles, and so on. He begins lecturing at the 'Free Literary Society'. In September, he attends the Zionist Congress in Basel. He sides with Dreyfus in the Dreyfus affair.

1898: Rudolf Steiner is very active as an editor in the political, artistic, and theatrical life of Berlin. He becomes friendly with John Henry Mackay and poet Ludwig Jacobowski (1868–1900). He joins Jacobowski's circle of writers, artists, and scientists—'The Coming Ones' (*Die Kommenden*)—and contributes lectures to the group until 1903. He also lectures at the 'League for College Pedagogy'. He writes an article for Goethe's sesquicentennial, 'Goethe's Secret Revelation,' on the 'Fairy Tale of the Green Snake and the Beautiful Lily'.

1898–99: 'This was a trying time for my soul as I looked at Christianity. . . . I was able to progress only by contemplating, by means of spiritual perception, the evolution of Christianity. . . . Conscious knowledge of real Christianity began to dawn in me around the turn of the century. This seed continued to develop. My soul trial occurred shortly before the beginning of the twentieth century. It was decisive for my soul's development that I stood spiritually before the Mystery of Golgotha in a deep and solemn celebration of knowledge.'

1899: Rudolf Steiner begins teaching and giving lectures and lecture cycles at the Workers' College, founded by Wilhelm Liebknecht (1826–1900). He will continue to do so until 1904. Writes: *Literature and Spiritual Life in the Nineteenth Century; Individualism in Philosophy; Haeckel and His Opponents; Poetry in the Present;* and begins what will become (fifteen years later) *The Riddles of Philosophy* (CW 18). He also meets many artists and writers, including Käthe Kollwitz, Stefan Zweig, and Rainer Maria Rilke. On October 31, he marries Anna Eunike.

1900: 'I thought that the turn of the century must bring humanity a new light. It seemed to me that the separation of human thinking and willing from the spirit had peaked. A turn or reversal of direction in human evolution seemed to me a necessity.' Rudolf Steiner finishes *World and Life Views in the Nineteenth Century* (the second part of what will become *The Riddles of Philosophy*) and dedicates it to Ernst Haeckel. It is published in March. He continues lecturing at *Die Kommenden*, whose leadership he assumes after the death of Jacobowski. Also, he gives the Gutenberg Jubilee lecture before 7,000 typesetters and printers. In September, Rudolf Steiner is invited by Count and Countess Brockdorff to lecture in the Theosophical Library. His first lecture is on Nietzsche. His second lecture is titled 'Goethe's Secret Revelation'. October 6, he begins a lecture cycle on the mystics that will become *Mystics after Modernism* (CW 7). November–December: 'Marie von Sivers appears in the audience....' Also in November, Steiner gives his first lecture at the Giordano Bruno Bund (where he will continue to lecture until May, 1905). He speaks on Bruno and modern Rome, focusing on the importance of the philosophy of Thomas Aquinas as monism.

1901:   In continual financial straits, Rudolf Steiner's early friends Moritz Zitter and Rosa Mayreder help support him. In October, he begins the lecture cycle *Christianity as Mystical Fact* (CW 8) at the Theosophical Library. In November, he gives his first 'Theosophical lecture' on Goethe's 'Fairy Tale' in Hamburg at the invitation of Wilhelm Hubbe-Schleiden. He also attends a gathering to celebrate the founding of the Theosophical Society at Count and Countess Brockdorff's. He gives a lecture cycle, 'From Buddha to Christ,' for the circle of the *Kommenden*. November 17, Marie von Sivers asks Rudolf Steiner if Theosophy needs a Western-Christian spiritual movement (to complement Theosophy's Eastern emphasis). 'The question was posed. Now, following spiritual laws, I could begin to give an answer....' In December, Rudolf Steiner writes his first article for a Theosophical publication. At year's end, the Brockdorffs and possibly Wilhelm Hubbe-Schleiden ask Rudolf Steiner to join the Theosophical Society and undertake the leadership of the German section. Rudolf Steiner agrees, on the condition that Marie von Sivers (then in Italy) work with him.

1902:   Beginning in January, Rudolf Steiner attends the opening of the Workers' School in Spandau with Rosa Luxemburg (1870–1919). January 17, Rudolf Steiner joins the Theosophical Society. In April, he is asked to become general secretary of the German Section of the Theosophical Society, and works on preparations for its founding. In July, he visits London for a Theosophical congress. He meets Bertram Keightly, G.R.S. Mead, A.P. Sinnett, and Annie Besant, among others. In September, *Christianity as Mystical Fact* appears. In October, Rudolf Steiner gives his first public lecture on Theosophy ('Monism and Theosophy') to about three hundred people at the Giordano Bruno Bund. On October 19–21, the German Section of the Theosophical Society has its first meeting; Rudolf Steiner is the general secretary, and Annie Besant attends. Steiner lectures on practical karma studies. On October 23, Annie Besant inducts Rudolf Steiner into the Esoteric School of the Theosophical Society. On October 25, Steiner begins a weekly series of lectures: 'The Field of Theosophy'. During this year, Rudolf Steiner also first meets Ita Wegman (1876–1943), who will become his close collaborator in his final years.

1903:   Rudolf Steiner holds about 300 lectures and seminars. In May, the first issue of the periodical *Luzifer* appears. In June, Rudolf Steiner visits

London for the first meeting of the Federation of the European Sections of the Theosophical Society, where he meets Colonel Olcott. He begins to write *Theosophy* (CW 9).

1904:   Rudolf Steiner continues lecturing at the Workers' College and elsewhere (about 90 lectures), while lecturing intensively all over Germany among Theosophists (about 140 lectures). In February, he meets Carl Unger (1878–1929), who will become a member of the board of the Anthroposophical Society (1913). In March, he meets Michael Bauer (1871–1929), a Christian mystic, who will also be on the board. In May, *Theosophy* appears, with the dedication: 'To the spirit of Giordano Bruno.' Rudolf Steiner and Marie von Sivers visit London for meetings with Annie Besant. June: Rudolf Steiner and Marie von Sivers attend the meeting of the Federation of European Sections of the Theosophical Society in Amsterdam. In July, Steiner begins the articles in *Luzifer-Gnosis* that will become *How to Know Higher Worlds* (CW 10) and *Cosmic Memory* (CW 11). In September, Annie Besant visits Germany. In December, Steiner lectures on Freemasonry. He mentions the High Grade Masonry derived from John Yarker and represented by Theodore Reuss and Karl Kellner as a blank slate 'into which a good image could be placed'.

1905:   This year, Steiner ends his non-Theosophical lecturing activity. Supported by Marie von Sivers, his Theosophical lecturing—both in public and in the Theosophical Society—increases significantly: 'The German Theosophical Movement is of exceptional importance.' Steiner recommends reading, among others, Fichte, Jacob Boehme, and Angelus Silesius. He begins to introduce Christian themes into Theosophy. He also begins to work with doctors (Felix Peipers and Ludwig Noll). In July, he is in London for the Federation of European Sections, where he attends a lecture by Annie Besant: 'I have seldom seen Mrs. Besant speak in so inward and heartfelt a manner....' 'Through Mrs. Besant I have found the way to H.P. Blavatsky.' September to October, he gives a course of thirty-one lectures for a small group of esoteric students. In October, the annual meeting of the German Section of the Theosophical Society, which still remains very small, takes place. Rudolf Steiner reports membership has risen from 121 to 377 members. In November, seeking to establish esoteric 'continuity,' Rudolf Steiner and Marie von Sivers participate in a 'Memphis-Misraim' Masonic ceremony. They pay forty-five marks for membership. 'Yesterday, you saw how little remains of former esoteric institutions.' 'We are dealing only with a "framework"... for the present, nothing lies behind it. The occult powers have completely withdrawn.'

1906:   Expansion of Theosophical work. Rudolf Steiner gives about 245 lectures, only 44 of which take place in Berlin. Cycles are given in Paris, Leipzig, Stuttgart, and Munich. Esoteric work also intensifies. Rudolf Steiner begins writing *An Outline of Esoteric Science* (CW 13). In January, Rudolf Steiner receives permission (a patent) from the Great Orient of the Scottish A & A Thirty-Three Degree Rite of the Order of the Ancient

Freemasons of the Memphis-Misraim Rite to direct a chapter under the name 'Mystica Aeterna'. This will become the 'Cognitive-Ritual Section' (also called 'Misraim Service') of the Esoteric School. (See: *Freemasonry and Ritual Work: The Misraim Service*, CW 265). During this time, Steiner also meets Albert Schweitzer. In May, he is in Paris, where he visits Edouard Schuré. Many Russians attend his lectures (including Konstantin Balmont, Dimitri Mereszkovski, Zinaida Hippius, and Maximilian Woloshin). He attends the General Meeting of the European Federation of the Theosophical Society, at which Col. Olcott is present for the last time. He spends the year's end in Venice and Rome, where he writes and works on his translation of H.P. Blavatsky's *Key to Theosophy*.

1907:   Further expansion of the German Theosophical Movement according to the Rosicrucian directive to 'introduce spirit into the world'—in education, in social questions, in art, and in science. In February, Col. Olcott dies in Adyar. Before he dies, Olcott indicates that 'the Masters' wish Annie Besant to succeed him: much politicking ensues. Rudolf Steiner supports Besant's candidacy. April-May: preparations for the Congress of the Federation of European Sections of the Theosophical Society—the great, watershed Whitsun 'Munich Congress,' attended by Annie Besant and others. Steiner decides to separate Eastern and Western (Christian-Rosicrucian) esoteric schools. He takes his esoteric school out of the Theosophical Society (Besant and Rudolf Steiner are 'in harmony' on this). Steiner makes his first lecture tours to Austria and Hungary. That summer, he is in Italy. In September, he visits Edouard Schuré, who will write the introduction to the French edition of *Christianity as Mystical Fact* in Barr, Alsace. Rudolf Steiner writes the autobiographical statement known as the 'Barr Document'. In *Luzifer-Gnosis*, 'The Education of the Child' appears.

1908:   The movement grows (membership: 1,150). Lecturing expands. Steiner makes his first extended lecture tour to Holland and Scandinavia, as well as visits to Naples and Sicily. Themes: St John's Gospel, the Apocalypse, Egypt, science, philosophy, and logic. *Luzifer-Gnosis* ceases publication. In Berlin, Marie von Sivers (with Johanna Mücke (1864–1949) forms the *Philosophisch-Theosophisch* (after 1915 *Philosophisch-Anthroposophisch*) *Verlag* to publish Steiner's work. Steiner gives lecture cycles titled *The Gospel of St John* (CW 103) and *The Apocalypse* (104).

1909:   *An Outline of Esoteric Science* appears. Lecturing and travel continues. Rudolf Steiner's spiritual research expands to include the polarity of Lucifer and Ahriman; the work of great individualities in history; the Maitreya Buddha and the Bodhisattvas; spiritual economy (CW 109); the work of the spiritual hierarchies in heaven and on earth (CW 110). He also deepens and intensifies his research into the Gospels, giving lectures on the Gospel of St Luke (CW 114) with the first mention of two Jesus children. Meets and becomes friends with Christian Morgenstern (1871–1914). In April, he lays the foundation stone for the Malsch model—the building that will lead to the first Goetheanum. In May, the International Congress of the Federation of European Sections of the

Theosophical Society takes place in Budapest. Rudolf Steiner receives the Subba Row medal for *How to Know Higher Worlds*. During this time, Charles W. Leadbeater discovers Jiddu Krishnamurti (1895–1986) and proclaims him the future 'world teacher,' the bearer of the Maitreya Buddha and the 'reappearing Christ'. In October, Steiner delivers seminal lectures on 'anthroposophy,' which he will try, unsuccessfully, to rework over the next years into the unfinished work, *Anthroposophy (A Fragment)* (CW 45).

1910:   New themes: *The Reappearance of Christ in the Etheric* (CW 118); *The Fifth Gospel; The Mission of Folk Souls* (CW 121); *Occult History* (CW 126); the evolving development of etheric cognitive capacities. Rudolf Steiner continues his Gospel research with *The Gospel of St Matthew* (CW 123). In January, his father dies. In April, he takes a month-long trip to Italy, including Rome, Monte Cassino, and Sicily. He also visits Scandinavia again. July–August, he writes the first mystery drama, *The Portal of Initiation* (CW 14). In November, he gives 'psychosophy' lectures. In December, he submits 'On the Psychological Foundations and Epistemological Framework of Theosophy' to the International Philosophical Congress in Bologna.

1911:   The crisis in the Theosophical Society deepens. In January, 'The Order of the Rising Sun,' which will soon become 'The Order of the Star in the East,' is founded for the coming world teacher, Krishnamurti. At the same time, Marie von Sivers, Rudolf Steiner's co-worker, falls ill. Fewer lectures are given, but important new ground is broken. In Prague, in March, Steiner meets Franz Kafka (1883–1924) and Hugo Bergmann (1883-1975). In April, he delivers his paper to the Philosophical Congress. He writes the second mystery drama, *The Soul's Probation* (CW 14). Also, while Marie von Sivers is convalescing, Rudolf Steiner begins work on *Calendar 1912/1913*, which will contain the 'Calendar of the Soul' meditations. On March 19, Anna (Eunike) Steiner dies. In September, Rudolf Steiner visits Einsiedeln, birthplace of Paracelsus. In December, Friedrich Rittelmeyer, future founder of the Christian Community, meets Rudolf Steiner. The *Johannes-Bauverein*, the 'building committee,' which would lead to the first Goetheanum (first planned for Munich), is also founded, and a preliminary committee for the founding of an independent association is created that, in the following year, will become the Anthroposophical Society. Important lecture cycles include *Occult Physiology* (CW 128); *Wonders of the World* (CW 129); *From Jesus to Christ* (CW 131). Other themes: esoteric Christianity; Christian Rosenkreutz; the spiritual guidance of humanity; the sense world and the world of the spirit.

1912:   Despite the ongoing, now increasing crisis in the Theosophical Society, much is accomplished: *Calendar 1912/1913* is published; eurythmy is created; both the third mystery drama, *The Guardian of the Threshold* (CW 14) and *A Way of Self-Knowledge* (CW 16) are written. New (or renewed) themes included life between death and rebirth and karma and reincarnation. Other lecture cycles: *Spiritual Beings in the Heavenly Bodies and in the Kingdoms of Nature* (CW 136); *The Human Being in the Light of Occultism, Theosophy, and Philosophy* (CW 137); *The Gospel of St Mark* (CW 139); and *The Bhagavad Gita and the Epistles of Paul* (CW 142). On May 8, Rudolf Steiner celebrates White Lotus Day, H.P. Blavatsky's death day, which he had faithfully observed for the past decade, for the last time. In August, Rudolf Steiner suggests the 'independent association' be called the 'Anthroposophical Society'. In September, the first eurythmy course takes place. In October, Rudolf Steiner declines recognition of a Theosophical Society lodge dedicated to the Star of the East and decides to expel all Theosophical Society members belonging to the order. Also, with Marie von Sivers, he first visits Dornach, near Basel, Switzerland, and they stand on the hill where the Goetheanum will be built. In November, a Theosophical Society lodge is opened by direct mandate from Adyar (Annie Besant). In December, a meeting of the German section occurs at which it is decided that belonging to the Order of the Star of the East is incompatible with membership in the Theosophical Society. December 28: informal founding of the Anthroposophical Society in Berlin.

1913:   Expulsion of the German section from the Theosophical Society. February 2–3: Foundation meeting of the Anthroposophical Society. Board members include: Marie von Sivers, Michael Bauer, and Carl Unger. September 20: Laying of the foundation stone for the *Johannes Bau* (Goetheanum) in Dornach. Building begins immediately. The third mystery drama, *The Soul's Awakening* (CW 14), is completed. Also: *The Threshold of the Spiritual World* (CW 147). Lecture cycles include: *The Bhagavad Gita and the Epistles of Paul* and *The Esoteric Meaning of the Bhagavad Gita* (CW 146), which the Russian philosopher Nikolai Berdyaev attends; *The Mysteries of the East and of Christianity* (CW 144); *The Effects of Esoteric Development* (CW 145); and *The Fifth Gospel* (CW 148). In May, Rudolf Steiner is in London and Paris, where anthroposophical work continues.

1914:   Building continues on the *Johannes Bau* (Goetheanum) in Dornach, with artists and co-workers from seventeen nations. The general assembly of the Anthroposophical Society takes place. In May, Rudolf Steiner visits Paris, as well as Chartres Cathedral. June 28: assassination in Sarajevo ('Now the catastrophe has happened!'). August 1: War is declared. Rudolf Steiner returns to Germany from Dornach—he will travel back and forth. He writes the last chapter of *The Riddles of Philosophy*. Lecture cycles include: *Human and Cosmic Thought* (CW 151); *Inner Being of Humanity between Death and a New Birth* (CW 153); *Occult Reading and Occult Hearing* (CW 156). December 24: marriage of Rudolf Steiner and Marie von Sivers.

1915:   Building continues. Life after death becomes a major theme, also art. Writes: *Thoughts during a Time of War* (CW 24). Lectures include: *The Secret of Death* (CW 159); *The Uniting of Humanity through the Christ Impulse* (CW 165).

1916:   Rudolf Steiner begins work with Edith Maryon (1872–1924) on the sculpture 'The Representative of Humanity' ('The Group'—Christ, Lucifer, and Ahriman). He also works with the alchemist Alexander von Bernus on the quarterly *Das Reich*. He writes *The Riddle of Humanity* (CW 20). Lectures include: *Necessity and Freedom in World History and Human Action* (CW 166); *Past and Present in the Human Spirit* (CW 167); *The Karma of Vocation* (CW 172); *The Karma of Untruthfulness* (CW 173).

1917:   Russian Revolution. The U.S. enters the war. Building continues. Rudolf Steiner delineates the idea of the 'threefold nature of the human being' (in a public lecture March 15) and the 'threefold nature of the social organism' (hammered out in May-June with the help of Otto von Lerchenfeld and Ludwig Polzer-Hoditz in the form of two documents titled *Memoranda*, which were distributed in high places). August–September: Rudolf Steiner writes *The Riddles of the Soul* (CW 20). Also: commentary on 'The Chymical Wedding of Christian Rosenkreutz' for Alexander Bernus (*Das Reich*). Lectures include: *The Karma of Materialism* (CW 176); *The Spiritual Background of the Outer World: The Fall of the Spirits of Darkness* (CW 177).

1918:   March 18: peace treaty of Brest-Litovsk—'Now everything will truly enter chaos! What is needed is cultural renewal.' June: Rudolf Steiner visits Karlstein (Grail) Castle outside Prague. Lecture cycle: *From Symptom to Reality in Modern History* (CW 185). In mid-November, Emil Molt, of the Waldorf-Astoria Cigarette Company, has the idea of founding a school for his workers' children.

1919:   Focus on the threefold social organism: tireless travel, countless lectures, meetings, and publications. At the same time, a new public stage of Anthroposophy emerges as cultural renewal begins. The coming years will see initiatives in pedagogy, medicine, pharmacology, and agriculture. January 27: threefold meeting: ' We must first of all, with the money we have, found free schools that can bring people what they need.' February: first public eurythmy performance in Zurich. Also: 'Appeal to the German People' (CW 24), circulated March 6 as a newspaper insert. In April, *Towards Social Renewal* (CW 23) appears— 'perhaps the most widely read of all books on politics appearing since the war'. Rudolf Steiner is asked to undertake the 'direction and leadership' of the school founded by the Waldorf-Astoria Company. Rudolf Steiner begins to talk about the 'renewal' of education. May 30: a building is selected and purchased for the future Waldorf School. August–September, Rudolf Steiner gives a lecture course for Waldorf teachers, *The Foundations of Human Experience (Study of Man)* (CW 293). September 7: Opening of the first Waldorf School. December (into January): first science course, the *Light Course* (CW 320).

1920:   The Waldorf School flourishes. New threefold initiatives. Founding of limited companies *Der Kommende Tag* and *Futurum A.G.* to infuse spiritual values into the economic realm. Rudolf Steiner also focuses on the sciences. Lectures: *Introducing Anthroposophical Medicine* (CW 312); *The Warmth Course* (CW 321); *The Boundaries of Natural Science* (CW 322); *The Redemption of Thinking* (CW 74). February: Johannes Werner

Significant Events in the Life of Rudolf Steiner * 191

Klein—later a co-founder of the Christian Community—asks Rudolf Steiner about the possibility of a 'religious renewal,' a 'Johannine church'. In March, Rudolf Steiner gives the first course for doctors and medical students. In April, a divinity student asks Rudolf Steiner a second time about the possibility of religious renewal. September 27–October 16: anthroposophical 'university course'. December: lectures titled *The Search for the New Isis* (CW 202).

1921:   Rudolf Steiner continues his intensive work on cultural renewal, including the uphill battle for the threefold social order. 'University' arts, scientific, theological, and medical courses include: *The Astronomy Course* (CW 323); *Observation, Mathematics, and Scientific Experiment* (CW 324); the *Second Medical Course* (CW 313); *Colour*. In June and September-October, Rudolf Steiner also gives the first two 'priests' courses' (CW 342 and 343). The 'youth movement' gains momentum. Magazines are founded: *Die Drei* (January), and—under the editorship of Albert Steffen (1884–1963)—the weekly, *Das Goetheanum* (August). In February–March, Rudolf Steiner takes his first trip outside Germany since the war (Holland). On April 7, Steiner receives a letter regarding 'religious renewal,' and May 22–23, he agrees to address the question in a practical way. In June, the Klinical-Therapeutic Institute opens in Arlesheim under the direction of Dr. Ita Wegman. In August, the Chemical-Pharmaceutical Laboratory opens in Arlesheim (Oskar Schmiedel and Ita Wegman are directors). The Clinical Therapeutic Institute is inaugurated in Stuttgart (Dr. Ludwig Noll is director); also the Research Laboratory in Dornach (Ehrenfried Pfeiffer and Günther Wachsmuth are directors). In November–December, Rudolf Steiner visits Norway.

1922:   The first half of the year involves very active public lecturing (thousands attend); in the second half, Rudolf Steiner begins to withdraw and turn toward the Society—'The Society is asleep.' It is 'too weak' to do what is asked of it. The businesses—*Der Kommende Tag* and *Futurum A.G.*—fail. In January, with the help of an agent, Steiner undertakes a twelve-city German lecture tour, accompanied by eurythmy performances. In two weeks he speaks to more than 2,000 people. In April, he gives a 'university course' in The Hague. He also visits England. In June, he is in Vienna for the East–West Congress. In August–September, he is back in England for the Oxford Conference on Education. Returning to Dornach, he gives the lectures *Philosophy, Cosmology, and Religion* (CW 215), and gives the third priests' course (CW 344). On September 16, The Christian Community is founded. In October–November, Steiner is in Holland and England. He also speaks to the youth: *The Youth Course* (CW 217). In December, Steiner gives lectures titled *The Origins of Natural Science* (CW 326), and *Humanity and the World of Stars: The Spiritual Communion of Humanity* (CW 219). December 31: Fire at the Goetheanum, which is destroyed.

1923:   Despite the fire, Rudolf Steiner continues his work unabated. A very hard year. Internal dispersion, dissension, and apathy abound. There is conflict—between old and new visions—within the Society. A wake-up call is needed, and Rudolf Steiner responds with renewed lecturing vitality. His focus: the spiritual context of human life; initiation science; the course of the year; and community building. As a foundation for an artistic school, he creates a series of pastel sketches. Lecture cycles: *The Anthroposophical Movement; Initiation Science* (CW 227) (in England at the Penmaenmawr Summer School); *The Four Seasons and the Archangels* (CW 229); *Harmony of the Creative Word* (CW 230); *The Supersensible Human* (CW 231), given in Holland for the founding of the Dutch society. On November 10, in response to the failed Hitler-Ludendorff putsch in Munich, Steiner closes his Berlin residence and moves the *Philosophisch-Anthroposophisch Verlag* (Press) to Dornach. On December 9, Steiner begins the serialization of his *Autobiography: The Course of My Life* (CW 28) in *Das Goetheanum*. It will continue to appear weekly, without a break, until his death. Late December–early January: Rudolf Steiner re-founds the Anthroposophical Society (about 12,000 members internationally) and takes over its leadership. The new board members are: Marie Steiner, Ita Wegman, Albert Steffen, Elisabeth Vreede, and Günther Wachsmuth. (See *The Christmas Meeting for the Founding of the General Anthroposophical Society*, CW 260). Accompanying lectures: *Mystery Knowledge and Mystery Centres* (CW 232); *World History in the Light of Anthroposophy* (CW 233). December 25: the Foundation Stone is laid (in the hearts of members) in the form of the 'Foundation Stone Meditation'.

1924:   January 1: having founded the Anthroposophical Society and taken over its leadership, Rudolf Steiner has the task of 'reforming' it. The process begins with a weekly newssheet ('What's Happening in the Anthroposophical Society') in which Rudolf Steiner's 'Letters to Members' and 'Anthroposophical Leading Thoughts' appear (CW 26). The next step is the creation of a new esoteric class, the 'first class' of the 'University of Spiritual Science' (which was to have been followed, had Rudolf Steiner lived longer, by two more advanced classes). Then comes a new language for Anthroposophy—practical, phenomenological, and direct; and Rudolf Steiner creates the model for the second Goetheanum. He begins the series of extensive 'karma' lectures (CW 235–40); and finally, responding to needs, he creates two new initiatives: biodynamic agriculture and curative education. After the middle of the year, rumours begin to circulate regarding Steiner's health. Lectures: January–February, *Anthroposophy* (CW 234); February: *Tone Eurythmy* (CW 278); June: *The Agriculture Course* (CW 327); June–July: *Speech Eurythmy* (CW 279); *Curative Education* (CW 317); August: (England, 'Second International Summer School'), *Initiation Consciousness: True and False Paths in Spiritual Investigation* (CW 243); September: *Pastoral Medicine* (CW 318). On September 26, for the first time, Rudolf Steiner cancels a lecture. On September 28, he gives his last lecture. On September 29, he withdraws to his studio in the carpenter's shop; now he is definitively ill. Cared for by Ita Wegman, he continues working, however, and writing the weekly installments of his *Autobiography* and *Letters to the Members/Leading Thoughts* (CW 26).

1925: Rudolf Steiner, while continuing to work, continues to weaken. He finishes *Extending Practical Medicine* (CW 27) with Ita Wegman.

On March 30, around ten in the morning, Rudolf Steiner dies.

INDEX